COMPACT
CYMRU

from C̶ ̶̶̶̶̶̶̶̶̶̶ ̶̶̶aris

Margaret Hughes
Illustrations: J. C. Davies

Gwasg Carreg Gwalch

First published in 2017
© text: Margaret Hughes
© images: J. C. Davies/Gwasg Carreg Gwalch
Cover image and images on pages 1, 4&5, 48, 99,
104, 105: © Crown copyright (2016) Visit Wales
© publication: Gwasg Carreg Gwalch 2017

ISBN: 978-1-84524-253-4
Cover design: Eleri Owen
Map: Alison Davies
Published by Gwasg Carreg Gwalch,
12 Iard yr Orsaf, Llanrwst, Wales LL26 0EH
tel: 01492 642031
website: www.carreg-gwalch.com

Acknowledgements

The author is grateful to many people for help in research . . . including Geraint Hughes, Faye Hughes, Eric Lander. Visitors of the past have written of their experiences, too, which have proved invaluable, too many to be listed here, but research through the internet will reveal their publications.

A book like this one would be nothing without illustrations. My thanks go to John C. Davies and John Cowell for valuable contributions which do so much to bring the stories to life.

Night descends on the Arfon villages

Contents

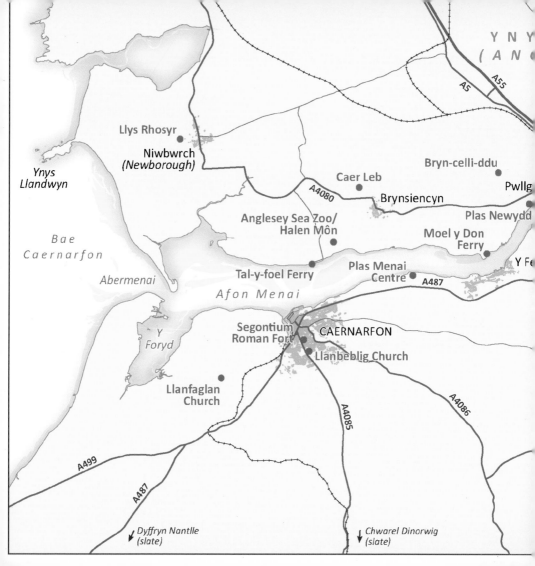

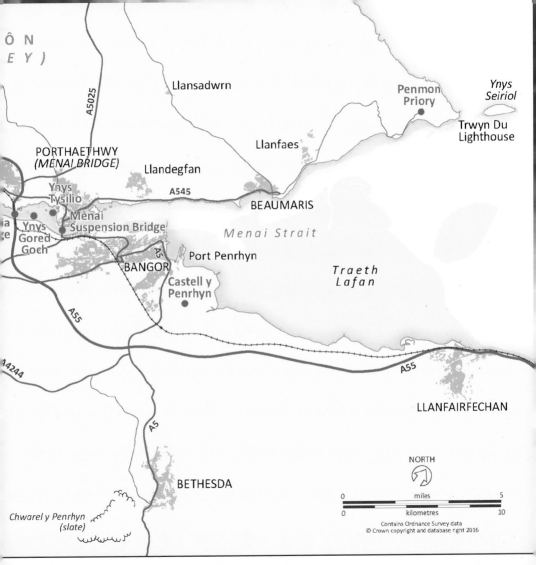

ÔN
EY)

Llansadwrn

Penmon
Priory

*Ynys
Seiriol*

Trwyn Du
Lighthouse

A5025

PORTHAETHWY
(MENAI BRIDGE)

Llanfaes

Llandegfan

A545

Ynys
Tysilio

Menai
Suspension Bridge

BEAUMARIS

Ynys
Gored
Goch

Menai Strait

Port Penrhyn

BANGOR

*Traeth
Lafan*

A5

Castell y
Penrhyn

A55

A4244

A55

LLANFAIRFECHAN

A5

BETHESDA

NORTH

*Chwarel y Penrhyn
(slate)*

| 0 | miles | 5 |
| 0 | kilometres | 10 |

Contains Ordnance Survey data
© Crown copyright and database right 2016

Introduction

The Menai Strait (*Afon Menai*), the narrow strip of water which divides Anglesey (*Ynys Môn*)from mainland Wales, is only twenty kilometres long, yet it boasts beautiful scenery. Many events of interest have happened here, and there have been some colourful characters.

This book is intended for the general reader, the visitor, or the new resident who wants to know something of the background to a new area, there is no other similar stretch of water in western Europe which compares with it.

The Strait is served by two tides, one from the east, the other from the west, which meet in between the Suspension and Britannia bridges. After a period of slack, they flow back to their original positions.

The sea bed is sharply rocky and can pose a hazard to navigators, however experienced they may be – they treat the Menai Strait with due respect.

Read on. The stories could colour both knowledge and enjoyment of the area. Future visits could be all the more attractive. Enjoy!

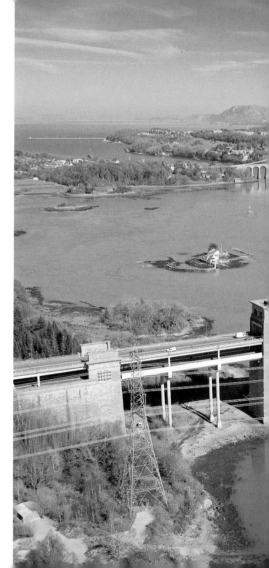

The Land of the Druids

As the ice sheets melted, the rising sea level created the Menai Strait, which has kept the people of Anglesey apart and unique over the years. Many of Wales' most ancient sites and monuments are in Anglesey, strongly suggesting that the earliest inhabitants came by sea. The remains of weapons and fishing hooks which date back well over 5,000 years have been found on Trwyn Du close to Afon Ffraw (*afon*: river).

With its western entrance facing towards the sunset, it is clear that sites along the Menai shoreline held a special significance to the early islanders. After c.3500 BC the tribes became more settled, and the mild climate made it possible to grow crops and cereals. The burial chambers of these early people can be found at Bodowyr, or Plas Newydd, and is significantly named as 'Bryn yr Hen Bobol' (*bryn*: mound; *hen bobol*: old people). Other examples of the burial chambers of that period in western Anglesey are the ones at Bryn-celli-ddu near Llanddaniel-fab, and Barclodiad y Gawres (the giantess'

apron) on the headland above the beach at Cable Bay (*Porth Trecastell*), in the direction of Rhosneigr. Inscribed stones at the Bryn-celli-ddu site suggest that the people had connections with Ireland and Brittany, and it appears that the site was used for many different purposes over the centuries. In Llansadwrn, on the land of Hen Drefor on the eastern side of Menai, are the remains of two burial chambers – the more westerly of which collapsed before 1770 and the one to the east following suit in 1825. These again belonged to a hazy era of time some four to six thousand years ago and the remains bear witness to the spiritual – and physical – strength of the inhabitants at that time.

It is thought that some of the *meini hirion* (standing stones) in Wales mark the burial place of a renowned leader or nobleman. A beaker was discovered at the foot of a *maen hir* (monolith) on the southern mainland, which strongly suggests that it is in fact a gravestone. Sometimes they seem to mark a path or route. Others are believed to be the

remains of stone circles which were part of the rituals of the druids. Towards Beaumaris, there is a *maen hir* which stands three metres high in a prominent position on the top of a small hill near Llandegfan. It is a striking location, with a view across the countryside for miles around, and the location holds a special atmosphere. But we do not know what its exact significance may have been.

Anglesey was obviously an important religious and cultural centre for the Celtic people in Wales. The treasures that have been found in places like Llyn Cerrig Bach on the island indicate that it was on the trading routes from Ireland to mainland Europe, and that influential leaders inhabited the island in the period 150–50 AD – which confirms that the island was the main centre of the druids of Britain. In 60 AD the Romans reached the shores of the Menai, and it is possible that they crossed the strait at Tal-y-foel, before destroying the sacred sites of the druids. After having to return south to defeat Boudica's (*Buddug*) forces, Julius Agricola and his legions returned to defeat the druids for the final time in 78 AD, and blood-curdling descriptions remain of the appearance and shrieks of the druids and their followers before this final confrontation.

A Roman Attack

The Romans had the most powerful army in the world. However, they feared the spiritual strength of the Celtic druids even more than their military strength. They had experienced that power in their campaigns against the tribes of Gaul (present-day France) and had been amazed by the hold the druids possessed over their people, in terms of politics, the law, literature, medicine as well as spirituality.

The Romans landed on the island of Britain in 43 AD. Several explanations have been offered for the invasion – the Romans' need for precious metals, for slaves and for fertile lands. However, it may be that their main motive was to quash the spiritual strength of the druids – and the centre of that religion was on Ynys Môn . The island was the site of oak trees and sacred groves where pagan ceremonies were held, as well as being the location of the 'druidic university' of western Europe.

The Romans marched towards north-western Wales in order to attack Môn, initially having been confronted by the fierce resistance of Caradog and his forces and then Boudica's rebellion. It became obvious to the Romans that they would have to attack Môn before they would be able to defeat the Celts. Around 60 BC, Paulinus prepared to attack the island, using flat-bottomed boats similar to coracles. The army had followed the Roman road from Caerhun (*Canovium*) in Dyffryn Conwy, over Bwlch y Ddeufaen and down to Abergwyngregyn and the shores of Traeth Lafan (*Lavan Sands*), opposite present-day Beaumaris. We know that Traeth Lafan was dry land at that time, apparently sinking below sea level in the 6th century.

Tacitus, one of Paulinus' soldiers, was the Romans' chronicler on that campaign. He recorded the fear evoked in them by the scene as they looked towards Môn:

'On the shore, the opposing army stood, a dense mass of armed men. Amongst the soldiers darted women dressed in black, like fiends, their hair wild, waving firebrands. The druids were everywhere, raising their arms to the heavens and hurling dreadful curses in our

Remains of Roman fort at Caer Leb

direction, frightening our soldiers. As a result, they stood completely still, as if all their joints had been paralysed by the strange scene . . . '

Eventually, the Roman general succeeded in restoring discipline among his troops and a great slaughter ensued on Anglesey. The Celtic warriors and their druids were killed as well as common folk. Others amongst them succeeded in escaping to Ireland and the Isle of Man and the sacred groves were destroyed by the Romans. It is very likely that the old religion continued to be practised secretly, as the druid tradition was an oral one and some say that their theology and philosophy influenced the early Celtic monastic church.

There is evidence from sites such as Castell Bryngwyn and Caer Leb that the Romans seized and adapted some the Celtic strongholds on the island for their own use. As well as exploiting the island's natural resources, such as the copper of Mynydd Parys, near Amlwch, the Romans would also have made use of the crops grown by the native farmers on the fertile lands leading down to the Menai. For over three hundred years after conquering Ynys Môn the Romans kept a beady eye on the island and its people from their fortress across the Menai at Segontium, or Caernarfon today, before they finally left the British Isles in 410 AD.

Cofis and Celts of Caernarfon

The castle on the quayside and the town walls cast long shadows – and you can read in the many guide books about the town that the inspiration came from the magnificent walls of Constantinople during its imperial days. In the Roman Museum at Segontium, the weapons carried by the legionaries who manned the fort (*caer*) still gleam and you can wander around the remains of the streets and barracks of this north-western outpost of the Roman empire. Street names such as Balaclava, Pretoria, Turkey Shore, Vinegar Hill and Waterloo remind us of the blood spilt in the name of the British Empire. Reminders of the old upholders of empire are difficult to avoid in Caernarfon.

And yet, in the pubs, in the market, at the Oval and on Coed Helen, the townspeople of Caernarfon, unique in so many ways and endearingly known as '*Cofis*', are to be found bantering and yelling in the Welsh language. On the hill at Twtil, there is an old Celtic hillfort.

A story is told of how a certain primary school teacher in Caernarfon was desperately trying to prise the word '*Celtiaid*' (Celts) from her class. 'Who built this fort before the Normans, before the English, before the Romans?' No answer. 'Who was here before all those people? The word begins with 'C'...?' A hand shot up. 'Yes?' '*Cofis*, Miss!'

The pupil was quite right, of course. Since prehistoric times, the Cofis are Celts, speaking Welsh, a Celtic language, and still adhering to the culture of those ancient Celtic tribes who were so influential throughout Europe for a whole millennium before the Romans came on the scene. The Celts created a cultural heritage through language and trading and they never had a military, colonial or civic empire as such – it wasn't a 'real' empire, according to some historians. But the ancient culture is found in its 21st century vibrant life in Caernarfon today, where it is difficult to take 'real' empires too seriously anyway!

1. Twtil, above Caernarfon and Menai; 2. Caernarfon from Twtil; 3. Roman town walls

Twtil is the highest point in Caernarfon – a small ochre-coloured outcrop which provides a superlative vantage point over the estuaries of Afon Seiont and Afon Menai, out to the undulating terrain of Môn (*Mona* to the Romans; *Anglesey* to the Vikings) and towards the chain of mountains stretching from Penmaen-mawr to Yr Eifl. In all weathers, in all seasons, the mountains form a formidable and dramatic backdrop – sometimes they are black, sometimes blue and sometimes purple. When the Celts reached Caernarfon, 2500 years ago, they too had a fort and watchtower on Twtil. Their name for the mountains was the name which is still used today – *Eryri* (Snowdonia) – 'the high mountains'. This was the home of the *eryr* (eagle), 'the high-flying bird'. Centuries later, the descendants of these Celts used the eryr as a symbol on their banners in the struggle to maintain the independence of the princes of Gwynedd. From the top of Twtil, several other Celtic forts are visible along the western coastline.

Among the main pleasures of the Celts were the recounting of legends and poetic composition. Some of the rich tradition of gods and wizards who walked the earth, has survived in Welsh. The most famous work in Wales' literary output is *Y Mabinogi*, a collection of myths and legends which are imbued with the richness of Celtic culture. The ancient kingdom of Gwynedd and the area around Caernarfon in particular provide the setting for some of the key events in these tales.

It was at Caer Saint (the local pronunciation of Afon Seiont, the river which flows into the Menai Strait below the castle), that Branwen's starling made its landfall, the winged messenger she sent from Ireland to complain to her brother Bendigeidfran about her ill-treatment at the hands of her husband. Math, the king of Gwynedd, had his main court at Caer Dathyl near Caernarfon, and there are other names such as Dôl Bebin, Bryn Gwydion and Caer Arianrhod which have strong links with the old legends.

1. *Segontium Roman fort at Caernarfon;*
2. & 3. *Latin inscribed stones and artefacts at the Roman museum*

Macsen and Elen

Caernarfon was one of the remotest outposts of the Roman Empire as it extended westwards. No visit to Caernarfon would be complete without calling at the Roman fort – Segontium – which lies about a mile from the centre of town on the Llanbeblig road on the way to Waunfawr and Beddgelert. In the museum at the site, there is a collection of pottery, coins and jewellery, discovered here by archaeologists between 1921 and 1923.

The military history of the caer can be divided into three phases; 75-140 AD; 210-290 AD and from early 350 to 380. The first caer was constructed of wood and incorporated a number of huts. At the beginning of the second century it was built of stone. For fifty years the great power of Rome was sufficient to keep the indigenous population under control. By the third phase of its history, the fort was an important administrative centre as well as a military base and its soldiers were allowed to intermarry with local women.

The design of the fort was modern for its period, parts of it being heated by a hypocaust. Another small caer was situated at Hen Walia on the Pwllheli road, but there is now very little of that fort to be seen.

After the exodus of the Romans towards the end of the 4th century, the caer fell into ruin, but there is evidence that a Welsh town had grown up in its place. Caernarfon is one of Wales' oldest towns and, in accordance with Welsh tradition, a large number of legends concerning the Welsh have accumulated around the old Roman forts.

The last Roman Governor at Segontium was Magnus Maximus, Macsen Wledig in Welsh. He originated from another Celtic land – Galicia, in the north-west of the Iberian peninsula – and he drew many of his legions from Britain during a struggle for the seat of power in Rome. According to legend, as a young soldier in Rome, he had dreamt of a fine fort in which there lived a beautiful. The dream was so vivid that he sent his men to

History in present day street names

the four corners of the earth to search for this fort. It was, of course, eventually found at Caernarfon, at the western entrance of Afon Menai. He was appointed governor and married the Celtic tywysoges, Elen Luyddog. At Elen's request, Macsen built several roads connecting different regions of Wales and parts of these roads are still known as Sarn Elen.

From being a man of empire Macsen became a fervent supporter of local autonomy. He united the tribes and created a strong nation in the land known today as Wales/Cymru. When he left the island of Britain in 383, Cymru was named as a country in its own right – and this is the date which has been appropriated as the date of the birth of the Welsh nation. *Y Ddraig Goch* (the red dragon) has been the flag of the Welsh since that time, the oldest national flag in the world.

Caer Gystennin was one of the old names for the fort at Caernarfon. Cystennin is Welsh for Constantinople, the magnificent city on the eastern fringes of the Roman Empire. Caernarfon still acknowledges Cystennin, Macsen and Elen with pride in the names of its streets and institutions.

A Nation of Saints

The *llannau* (pl. of *llan*, enclosed ground, churchyard) on the shores of Menai are named after early Celtic saints who originally established the churches there: Baglan (Llanfaglan), Peblig (Llanbeblig, Caernrafon), Edwen (Llanedwen), Nidan (Llanidan), Tegfan (Llandegfan) and Sadwrn (Llansadwrn). Others gave their names to islands where they lived in hermit cells as the islands of Seiriol (*Puffin Island*), Llanddwyn (after Dwynwen, the saint of Welsh lovers) and Tysilio indicate. Saint Deiniol established his religious centre in Bangor, and in 546 AD Prince Maelgwn of Gwynedd consecrated Deiniol as Bishop of Bangor, and thereby establishing, by all accounts, the oldest see on mainland Britain. Bangor developed into a centre that nurtured numerous saints, and their names are still with us today in the names of the churches and parishes of the area.

The most influential saint on the north-eastern shore was Seiriol. His ecclesiastical centre was in Penmon and the remains of the original 6th century buildings can be seen there. A number of carved stones and Celtic crosses from the age of the saints have been preserved. The church and the monastery at Penmon received patronage from the Welsh princes, including Owain Gwynedd and Llywelyn Fawr. The remains of Seiriol's original cell and well are still to be seen on the site, and on the island named after him are the remains of another monastery dating back to the 12th century.

This was the era known in Wales as the Age of the Saints, when the Celtic Church was established with its own autonomous style and beliefs,

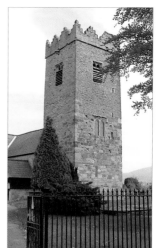

Llanbeblig church

its monks adhering much more closely to nature and a simple way of life than the episcopal church which developed in Rome.

Llanbeblig, in the shadow of the fort at Segontium, is the parish church at Caernarfon to this day. Peblig, *Publicum* in Latin, was, according to tradition, one of Macsen Wledig's sons. Whether or not this is true, the experts are certain that this has been a Christian site since the beginning of the 5th century – some two centuries before Saint Austin was sent from Rome to England as a missionary among the pagan Saxons.

Today, Llanbeblig bears few of the characteristics of the early Celtic church. The upper portion of the tower dates from the 16th century and it is unusual because of its battlements. At one time, the church would have been lime-washed as a landmark for ships heading for the quayside. The screen has disappeared, but the discovery of burial remains in the graveyard and an old altar in the church dating back to the Roman period testify to this having been consecrated ground since that time.

A much simpler church, but one which has a lot more character, is the old church of Llanfaglan near Foryd Fawr. The oldest parts of the building date back to the 13th century and it has not suffered 'restoration' at the hands of the Victorians – the pews and pulpit remain unchanged since the 18th century. An old inscribed stone in the door lintel dates back to the 5th or 6th century.

The ancient church of St Mary's, part of which is embedded in the town walls, stands within the old fortified borough of Caernarfon. This was the church of the Norman garrison in the castle and it was originally built by Henry de Ellerton c.1307-1316. There is a vestry in the roof which looks out across Afon Menai, and at one time, it seems the tower served a military purpose as well as providing quarters for the castle chaplain. In this church, the presiding judge would hold a service every time the Quarter Sessions convened in the town. One of the church's treasures is 'Jesse's window', but the old wooden rood screen no longer exists here either – it went on sale in 1829 and was described as being 'suitable' for firewood.

Ynys Tysilio

A little to the west along the Strait from Ynys y Moch and hugging the Anglesey shore, lies Ynys Tysilio, or *Church Island*. Walk down the tree-lined lane which separates the bridge from the Anglesey Arms hotel and you enter another world. Traffic on the bridge is silenced.

At the foot of the hill an opening on the right leads to a pleasant promenade, the Belgian Walk, built by Flemish refugees during the First World War, to give them employment. This gives extensive views of the Strait and the bridges, ending in a causeway which is the entrance to Ynys Tysilio.

Tysilio was a missionary, the younger son of a 7th century king of Powys. Unlike his elder brother, who was aristocratic and warlike, Tysilio had a more gentle disposition, and studied under a Christian leader of his day. He came to north Wales, seeking seclusion, somewhere he could pray and meditate in peace, and found it on this small island. He set up his cell, later building a small church on the site which, in turn, was enlarged during the 15th century. A stone embedded in one wall carried the date 630. More development took place during the 19th century using much of the original stone.

The roof has three medieval trusses, the soffits of which are curved and chamfered. The windows on the north and south walls are relatively modern, but the east window is a reproduction of a 15th century window. The gable coping and a cross socket have been dated to the 15th century and the font to the 14th. 'Saint' Tysilio's church is now only used on special occasions. The parish church of St Mary, Porthaethwy (*Menai Bridge*), stands on the steep rise on the A5 near the Anglesey entrance to the suspension bridge.

The island church is surrounded by an extensive graveyard, the final resting place of local inhabitants, and others, over the centuries. Servants to local wealthy families, those who died tragically at sea, all are remembered here. The graves all add to the tranquil atmosphere of the island.

Ynys Tysilio

From the graveyard a pathway meanders around the island shore. From here, one can look out west over the dangerous water of the Strait, to Robert Stephenson's railway bridge, originally a famous structure of iron tubes. During the 1970s a disastrous fire destroyed them, and the bridge was rebuilt, with an open rail track and a road bridge above it. This is now the A55 expressway.

Over marshland to the north of Ynys Tysilio in the nesting season, terns, shags, cormorants and gulls gather in their hundreds – a sight always popular with birdwatchers.

Submerged rocks and whirlpools combined with dangerous tides, make navigation through the Strait difficult, especially around the Swellies rocks which now carry a buoy to warn approaching vessels of the hazards. Sailing through here is an adventure, only to be attempted by those with the necessary knowledge. What did Tysilio make of it, we wonder.

Ynys Seiriol

(*Priestholm* or *Puffin Island*)

Ynys Seiriol is a hump of limestone a mile long, lying only a very short distance from Penmon, on mainland Anglesey. Access can be difficult, due to turbulent water and tidal flow. The channel is very narrow.

After visiting Ynys Seiriol during the latter half of the 16th century, William Worcester in *Itinerarium* describes it as being 'separated from the mainland as by the distance covered by the flight of two arrows with bow shots' and records seeing its surface 'covered with elder trees'. He found rabbits and adders there.

There was once a great colony of puffins, hence the English name, but a count in 1990 revealed only thirty pairs. That same count also revealed four hundred cormorants breeding – over half the Welsh cormorant population. There was also a colony of kittiwakes.

When puffins were abundant, they were caught and pickled packed in barrels and sent to the cities where they were considered a delicacy. Then a persistent colony of brown rats searching for eggs among nesting seabirds, has been blamed for the decrease in numbers.

Grey seals sometimes rest on the foreshore of the island. They are an attraction to tourists who take the occasional boat trip from Beaumaris to see them.

The effect of *myxamatosis* prevalent through Britain in 1954-5 changed the pattern of plant life on Ynys Seiriol because of absence of rabbits.

An early religious settlement, founded by 'Saint' Seiriol in the 7th century became a monastery and later a church. The monastery was of the Augustinian order. It is not known how many were in that early settlement. Burials took place there, as graves have been found. Seiriol's original sanctuary became the monastery church. Its tower remains.

When the semaphore signal system was set up to carry maritime messages from Holyhead (*Caergybi*) to the Liverpool warehouses, a station was sited on Ynys Seiriol. Signals were relayed from here to

Ynys Tysilio

the Orme at Llandudno, then along the line to the Wirral. The system ceased to be used when modern telegraphic techniques came into popularity, and the building was taken over by the Liverpool Marine Biology Committee and used as a laboratry. This was later moved to the Isle of Man, but the remains of the building on the island remind us of its previous uses.

Ynys Seiriol has always been regarded as a mystical place. Legends telling us of lands below the sea have always been a part of folklore.

Traeth Lafan, just off the coast, has its tales to tell. At very low tide, 'walls' are seen protruding which, for centuries, have been regarded as part of a lost city. But scientists say they are merely accumulations of stone left from the Ice Age. So much for imagination.

Deiniol's Cathedral at Bangor

Bangor was placed on the map when Saint Deiniol chose it as the site of his sanctuary in the 6th century. The Emperor Constantine officially recognised Christianity as one of the established religions of the Roman empire in 313 AD, and Bangor was on one of the Romans' main routes through Wales. After the Roman legions left for home, Cunedda and his sons from 'Yr Hen Ogledd' ('the Old North'), the northern regions of England and southern Scotland, came down to northern Wales to maintain the Roman order, and Celtic Christianity used the western seaways to extend its influence over the region.

The Menai Strait was an important channel for the saints. Deiniol himself was a descendent of the royal house of Rheged in northern Britain. After being influenced by the saints' evangelical movement, he established his cell in the valley of Afon Adda in 525 AD. His cell developed into a centre for training missionaries, and its circle of round huts within a wooden pallisade gave the name 'Bangor' to the city which grew in the valley, and which became the most important religious centre in northern Wales.

In 546 AD Maelgwn, the king of Gwynedd, made Deiniol the first Bishop of Bangor, establishing the oldest Bishopric on mainland Britain. According to tradition, while at Bangor, Maelgwn was converted to Christianity, and confessed all his sins. Maelgwn died of the yellow fever in 560 AD, but before dying he gave the Bishop of Bangor lands and rights, and he set in motion the process of building the 'Greater Bangor in Arfon'. Maelgwn was buried on Ynys Seiriol.

Deiniol died c.584 but the connection with the kings of Gwynedd remained. As part of his campaign to create a strong and settled Gwynedd in the 12th century, Gruffudd ap Cynan and his Bangor Bishop began the work of building a new stone cathedral at Bangor, and a few remains of that early building can still be seen within the modern church. Gruffudd's son and

1. & 3. Bangor cathedral; 2. How Bangor may have looked in the 6th-7th century

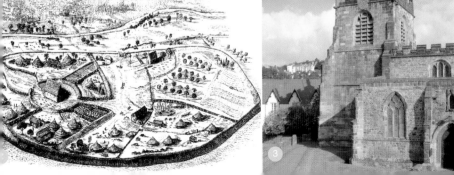

Archaeological finds at Abergwyngregyn

heir, Owain Gwynedd, continued this work, and the fact that both Gruffudd and Owain are buried close to the main altar indicates the importance of the relationship between the princes of Gwynedd and the see of Bangor. The coat of arms of both princes can be seen on two of the choir stalls in the cathedral.

Owain's reign was a period of constant opposition to the power and influence of the English crown. In 1157 Owain had a famous victory over the forces of Henry II at Tâl Moelfre, or Moel-y-Don today, on Anglesey, 'and at tâl Moelfre a thousand banners' were the words of the poet Gwalchmai in his eulogy to Owain. When he died, Owain Gwynedd left a strong kingdom, and the *tywysog* (prince) of Gwynedd was the only Welsh leader with the right to be called *tywysog*. But in the subsequent years, feuds developed between his sons, and King John of England took advantage of Gwynedd's relative weakness at the time, and burnt

Bangor, and the cathedral, to the ground in 1210.

The main court of the princes of Gwynedd was at Aberffraw on Anglesey, but they also had another important stronghold at the eastern end of the Menai Strait, at Abergwyngregyn, a stone's throw from Bangor. By the early years of the 13th century, Owain Gwynedd's grandson, Llywelyn ap Iorwerth, had gained control of the whole of Gwynedd. In 1205, Llywelyn married Siwan (or Joan), the daughter of King John. He died in a monk's habit at Aberconwy Abbey in 1240. In the meantime, Llywelyn had succeeded to build a strong, united Gwynedd, and had established himself as the undisputed overlord of all Wales' native leaders.

The next, and last tywysog, to establish a secure Gwynedd, and to be officially recognised as *Tywysog Cymru* (the Prince of Wales) in 1267, was Llywelyn ap Gruffudd. The cathedral at Bangor flourished during his reign. Bishop Anian I further extended the building, and it is quite probable that he was responsible for one of the treasures of the cathedral, *Anian's Pontifical*, now in the care of the University Library at Bangor. The beautiful illuminated manuscript is another indication of the way the cathedral thrived during the time of the Welsh princes.

The cathedral was extended in the 14th century and a west wing added. The tower had been burnt again in 1309 and that particular tower was never rebuilt. But the 14th century was not a pleasant time in Wales. There was an increasing rift between the church and the Welsh population after the fall of the Welsh princes. The English crown tended to appoint English bishops.

During the early years of his rebellion, it is apparent that Owain Glyndŵr agreed with the opposition to the Anglisized church, and his forces torched the cathedral at Bangor in 1402. As Glyndŵr restored the power of the old Welsh princes however, the old relationship with the church at Bangor was re-established. Lewys ab Ieuan and Gruffudd Yonge, both bishops of Bangor in their day, were also close counsellors to Glyndŵr. Gruffudd Yonge was also in all probability one of the masterminds behind the ideal of establishing an independent Church and University in Wales, an ideal that was finally realised at Bangor at the beginning of the 20th century.

Snowdonia from Anglesey

Resisting the Chains and the Castles

Two Norman castles and two Norman colonial towns were built at Caernarfon and Beaumaris by Edward I to try and subdue and control the Welsh population of the 13th Century. Today, they stand tall and magnificent, but their actual effect on late medieval history was more propaganda than military.

As early as 1090, Huw Flaidd ('Hugh the Wolf'), the Norman Earl of Chester, managed to carve a route for himself along the coast of northern Wales and to occupy Caernarfon. He built a motte and bailey castle at the strong defensive position between Afon Seiont, Afon Cadnant and Afon Menai. He didn't get to stay long. Under the leadership of Gruffudd ap Cynan, the Cymry rose up and sent him packing back over Offa's Dyke. They then occupied the site, building something akin to the castles at Dolbadarn or Dolwyddelan with a town growing up around it. Both Llywelyn lived here, and land and trading rights from the port at Aber Saint were given to the inhabitants. Thus, long before there was any mention of Edward I, Caernarfon had been a town of princes, and was beginning to develop its own character.

Having set aside vast resources and an army of mercenaries from all over Europe to defeat the last princes of Gwynedd, Edward I decided to put his stamp on Caernarfon. This had been one of the farthest-flung corners of the Roman Empire which had remained unconquered since the departure of Macsen Wledig some 900 years previously in 383. Here, in the shadow of the mountains of Eryri, where Celtic gods and kings reigned, where the eagle of proud Rome had flown in the wind, he built a castle and a town which would be embodied in the mythology of the area. With its angular towers and bands of sandstone, the design of the castle reflects that of the palace at Constantinople in the east, and this was no fluke. One of the main towers was called Tŵr yr Eryr (*the eagle tower*) and it

1. Caernarfon castle above the Menai;
2. & 3. Its powerful town walls and towers

was adorned by eagles carved from stone. This was the most expensive of Edward I's castles and its magnificence and strength were a symbol of the great imperial power he imagined he possessed. The Welsh were evicted from the town to make way for the walls of the new settlement. This was colonised by foreigners from England and their privileges and rights were denied to the Welsh.

The castle and town of Caernarfon represented oppression to the Welsh and that is why it took forty years to build. In 1294, ten years after Edward I gave his royal charter to the town of Caernarfon, the Welsh rose up in rebellion, attacking and burning the town. The castle fell into their hands and remained in their possession for six months. They knew Edward and his army would return, so they spent that time demolishing the thick walls of the town.

This was a national revolt, with castles and towns throughout Wales being seized or razed to the ground by the Welsh, and several of the leaders joined forces in the fight for freedom. The leader in the north of the country was Madog ap Llywelyn of Meirionnydd, and he was recognised as the Prince of Wales by the other leaders. Edward I led his vast army and navy to Wales but Madog is reputed to have kept up the morale of his men by means of his magnificent patriotic oratory. Edward I found himself besieged in Conwy castle and the great imperial monarch was, for a while, obliged to live on meagre rations of honey and water. More forces poured in from England and Madog and his soldiers were defeated in a battle in central Wales. Madog was incarcerated in 1295 and was imprisoned for the rest of his days in the Tower of London.

During Madog's revolt, the Welsh manifested their hatred of the foreign rule which had been imposed upon them by Edward, by hanging the town sheriff, Roger de Pulesdon, from the upstairs window of his own house in Stryd y Plas, Caernarfon. All the treasury records in Porth Mawr, the administrative and financial centre for north-western Wales, were burnt and the English sheriff of Anglesey was killed.

Twll yn y Wal ('hole in the wall')
– a monument to Madog's revolt

On a Beautiful Marsh

Having licked his wounds from these incursions, Edward was more determined than ever to hold on to his empire. He commissioned a new castle and colony at Beaumaris (Norman French for '*beautiful marsh*') on the far side of the Menai Strait. He repaired and strengthened the walls of Caernarfon castle. Punitive legislation was passed against the Welsh, making them slaves in their own country. Wales is the most castled land in Europe and Edward's castles and towns were the largest and most expensive building project in Europe during the Middle Ages.

Beaumaris castle was built between 1295 and 1298, creating an important link with Caernarfon on the banks of Afon Menai and Conwy further along the coast to the east. The castle has a unique, concentric design – it is a castle within a castle. The defences are further testimony to the strength of the Welsh resistance at the time.

Its construction required an enormous army of 1,000 labourers, 400 craftsmen and 200 carters who transported the stones mainly from Penmon quarry. Originally, the castle moat was connected to the sea so that ships could sail directly from Afon Menai to the safety of the castle walls.

The town was established outside the castle but within the external walls of the settlement. Edward's intention, as always, was to encourage English people to live there and to keep the Welsh out. Land was taken from the Welsh and given rent-free for ten years to incomers to grow crops and rear animals. It was English law which was administered in the towns and the Welsh did not have the right to be on a jury. The Welsh language was prohibited and the English were forbidden to marry the Welsh. Welsh farmers and craftsmen had to bring their goods and produce to the town market, which was held outside the walls, and sell them for prices set by the colonists. According to one legend, Edward I held a feast in Beaumaris castle, inviting some 300 Welsh poets to attend – the poets were the spiritual leaders of the people, like the druids of old. In the middle of the feast, according to the legend, Edward's soldiers attacked the guests, killing all the poets.

Edward's scheme of centralising governmental power, military strength and commercial wealth in the castles and the new boroughs, thereby turning Wales into a colony of the English throne, was ineffectual. Even in 1305, the Welsh owned a great deal of property in the town and in that year, a Welshman was the richest man in Beaumaris.

Beaumaris castle

Rhosyr and Newborough dunes

On the banks of the Menai, Edward I's architect, James of St George, built towering castles in Caernarfon and Beaumaris, overturning the sites of Llywelyn's courts at Aberffraw and Abergwyngregyn. In order to completely remove any signs of the old order, the stones and beams of Aberffraw were used in the construction of Caernarfon castle. And the castle at Beaumaris was built within a stone's throw of the Welsh port of Llan-faes, the largest town in Gwynedd in the 13th century, and the place where the Welsh princesses Siwan (Joan) and Eleanor, wife of Llywelyn the Last, were buried.

Where a castle was built, an English town would be established. Most of the citizens would be from the English marches primarily, with a few others attracted there from Ireland, Gascony and Savoy. An area of approximately 1,500 hectares around the new town would be cleared of all its native Welsh inhabitants, to create arable land to grow crops and keep animals to feed the garrison, as well as to keep a clear space with good visibility around the town walls. Llan-faes fell within this area, and as a result, as they built Beaumaris castle, all the Welsh inhabitants of Llan-faes were forcibly moved to the Rhosyr area. In 1303 this new township received its charter and was called 'New Borough', which has become Niwbwrch in Welsh, and it remains one of the largest Welsh-speaking areas on Anglesey.

This resulted in a dramatic change in the lives of the people who had to move. Instead of the comparative wealth of Llan-faes and the surrounding countryside, from now on they had to survive in a land of sand dunes, beaches and saltmarsh, and the continual prevailing winds from the south-west always threatened to extend the dunes towards the farmlands. Throughout the period up to the reign of Elizabeth I the sands threatened the village of Niwbwrch. During a great storm in 1330, 211 acres of land were covered by sands swept by the wind, including the remains of the old court of Rhosyr.

The local population proved very stubborn however, mastering new skills such as fishing, boatbuilding and quarrying, as well as farming the good land. Another craft developed in the Niwbwrch area as a result of the local landscape. The sea-sedges, or reeds which grew on the dunes and anchored them were harvested by the local women, and then the spiny green leaves were used to make brooms, brushes for whitewashing walls, baskets, nets and ropes. They were also weaved into strips which were tied together to make floormats or covers for hayricks. The local farmers would pay the women for their work and in later times they succeeded in finding a wider market

The rediscovered site of Rhosyr court

Owain Glyndŵr on Menai's shores

The next national leader to visit Caernarfon and to rekindle the fire of independence in the hearts of his fellow countrymen was Owain Glyndŵr, the national hero of Wales. In a long campaign for independence which lasted over 15 years, Owain attacked every English castle and borough in Wales in the face of the greatest military power in the world at the time.

He established a government for Wales; he dreamed of an education system, an independent church for Wales and re-establishing Welsh as the official national language.

On 2nd November, 1401, a small Welsh army appeared on the summit of the ancient Celtic fort at Twtil. They were led by Owain Glyndŵr, who had already been proclaimed as Prince of Wales by his supporters. For over a year, his army had been attacking a chain of English castles and towns throughout Wales, razing them to the ground. He had won a great victory at the battle of Hyddgen that summer and his war of independence had spread to every corner of Wales.

He reached Caernarfon, raising his golden dragon banner at the head of his forces for the first time. Another of his heraldic symbols was four red and yellow lions which had strong associations with the tywysogion of Gwynedd. He attacked the town and set fire to it, but a small group of soldiers managed to shut themselves within the safety of the castle. The constable of the castle was killed,

1 The princely seal of Owain Glyndŵr (National Museum of Wales)

A replica of Owain Glyndŵr's great seal on display in Welsh castles today

however, by an arrow from the bow of one of Owain's men.

In 1400, during this great rebellion, the Welsh of Anglesey, under the leadership of the Tudors of Penmynydd, attacked Henry IV and his army in Rhos Fawr near Beaumaris, forcing them to retreat to the safety of the castle. The castle was under heavy siege in 1402 and 1403 and a fleet from England had to be sent to reinforce it. In January 1404, the sheriff of Anglesey was captured and 200 of his retinue were killed when he attempted to leave the safety of Beaumaris castle and travel across the island. Later that year, Glyndŵr's army occupied the castle for a while, before establishing Harlech and Aberystwyth as headquarters for his campaign. In the summer of 1405, it is recorded that one of the English military objectives was 'to go to Anglesey and recover the castle of Beaumaris'.

1404 was a great year for Glyndŵr and capturing the last castle which Edward built in Wales was a huge feather in his cap. It is no wonder that he has been an inspiration to the Welsh for over 600 years.

Later on, Owain held a series of independent national parliaments. Ambassadors would come from European countries to see him, and he had plans for an independent church and university in Wales. He kept his rebellion going for some 15 years despite the immense power mustered against him by the English king, before disappearing from the history books into the world of myth and legend. It is not known where Glyndŵr died but his great dream lives on.

It is the influence of those who were incarcerated in the castle rather than those who built it which has lived on. Neither Caernarfon or Beaumaris castles were put to any great military use, and in 1660, an order came from Charles II that Caernarfon should be demolished, but the order was ignored, and so it still stands to this day above the ebb and flow of Afon Menai, a picturesque monument and a symbol of an unyielding spirit. Edward's aim was to bury the spirit and dreams of the Welsh forever, but rather than being symbols of conquest and imperial power, the castles and their stone ramparts became a memorial to the resilience of the Welsh nation.

Ports of Caernarfon

Abermenai has been a port since the days of the *Mabinogi*, and there is evidence that the old Roman fort at Hen Walia was built to protect the galleys anchored in the harbour below from Irish pirates. Trading vessels and fishing boats would also use the quay in Roman times.

The quay was an important part of Edward I's grand scheme since his new castle was already protected on three sides by deep moats. With his navy, the town and keep could be supplied from the sea when they were hard pressed. It seems that Edward had no intention of trying to control the mountains – merely to secure footholds and make a show of strength along the coast.

Nowadays, the boats on the Seiont estuary and in the Marina at Cei Bach or Doc Fictoria are mostly pleasure craft. There are a few local fishing vessels still to be seen, and one of the grand old sailing ships which used to set sail from Caernarfon for ports in the far corners of the globe. It is not difficult to imagine the bustling activity on the foreshore and the local lads eyeing up the ships loading at the quayside, yearning for a life of adventure at sea. In the words of the well-known Welsh folksong:

> 'O *na chawn i fynd ar f'union*
> *Dros y môr a hwylio'n ôl i G'narfon.'*
> (Why can't I go to sea right away
> sailing back to Caernarfon some day.)

The offices of the Harbourmaster, built at the same time as Cei Llechi (*cei*: quay; *llechi*: slate) in 1846, are still standing. The Anglesey public house is outside the town walls on the other side of the castle – at one time this was the customs house for the port and it still belongs to the harbour trust, although it has been a public house since 1822. In 1845 and 1846, Lord Newborough hosted two successful regattas on Afon Menai and the following year the Royal Welsh Yacht Club was formed. Since 1854, that club has been

1. Cei Llechi from across the estuary;
2. A pleasure boat entering the harbour

housed in one of the towers on the promenade which is called the South of France by the Cofis.

There used to be a very special maritime school in the town at one time – run by another remarkable woman called Elen – Ellen Edwards. It drew prospective sailors from all parts of northern Wales and it is estimated that over a thousand sailors attended classes at the school between 1830 and 1889.

Cei Bach was built in the 1870s with the intention of extending the harbour all the way from Cei Llechi to Yr Ala Las on the eastern edge of town. There was a flour mill and a shipyard here during the old days and early on in its history, lights were placed around the quay due to the tendency of drunken sailors to fall into the water and drown as they tried to negotiate their way back to their ships after a night in the pubs of Caernarfon. On the outer wall of the quay, the landing stage used in the old days by the ferry from Brynsiencyn in Anglesey can still be seen.

The sea around these shores offered a livelihood, but also at times took lives. This was especially true of the ferry which crossed the Menai from Tal-y-foel to Y Felinheli. Seventy-nine passengers were killed when the ferry capsized in 1664, and a further thirty drowned in 1723. In 1785 the Abermenai ferry got into difficulties in rough seas near Caernarfon and fifty-four passengers drowned. One passenger, Huw Williams, managed to escape with his life. The name must be a lucky one, for a man of the same name survived the sinking of another ferry, the one from Barras, in 1820, when twenty-two passengers died.

Also on the edge of the quay stands the Maritime Museum, which brings together some of the port's heritage.

1. Cei Bach; 2.The Maritime Museum at Cei Bach;
3. The Harbourmaster building at Cei Llechi

Beaumaris Port

The age of the Tudors was a prosperous period for many gentry in Wales – the punitive laws against the Welsh were eventually abolished, making it possible for them to hold influential office, control the commerce of the towns and start to develop the country's industries. Sadly, this turn of fortune drew some of these families closer to the ways of London, in effect they became foreign landlords, who chose to refute the social and cultural duties which were expected of them under the old Welsh order.

In Beaumaris the Bulkeleys were the influential family. There is a wonderful 15th century alabaster cist grave in the parish church of Beaumaris, for William Bulkeley and his wife Elen, who was related to the Tudors. The cist grave was originally in the monastery of Llan-faes but it was moved to the church in the town when the monastery was dissolved during Henry VIII's reign. It is believed that the choir stalls also came from Llan-faes. Baron Hill, now a ruin, was the Bulkeley family home.

Trade in the town flourished in the late Middle Ages. The oldest residential building is the Tudor Rose, a wooden-framed house from the early 15th century, which is now a shop. It reflects the town's prosperity in a period when Beaumaris became the most important port in north-western Wales. Fishing was the mainstay of the economy – there was a fish farm and several weirs on the Menai by the end of the 15th century. This was the port which connected the mainland with Anglesey and when the quarries of Arfon began to be developed during the age of Elizabeth I, the port of Beaumaris was exporting slates to Eire and Chester, returning with a cargo of wine and Irish linen.

When trade with the Caribbean islands began to increase in the 17th century, Beaumaris grew to become the main port of northern Wales for importing tobacco and sugar. Ships on their way to Liverpool would anchor in Beaumaris bay and transfer some of their cargo to smaller

The Menai shore at Beaumaris

boats which would sail along the coast. The port had the natural advantage of being one of the most sheltered parts on the coast between Cornwall and southern Scotland.

The bay was also deep – the disadvantage of the ports of Conwy and Caernarfon was that they were on estuaries. When lead began to be mined in the Conwy valley, it was Beaumaris rather than Conwy which was chosen as a port for exporting the ore to Germany.

Traeth Lafan
– an early crossing point of the Strait

The eastern end of the Menai Strait is marked by an extensive area of flat sandbank, known as Traeth Lafan, covered during a high tide, but visible at an ebb. This provided an early crossing point for travellers from the mainland, making for Anglesey and Holyhead and the sea crossing to Ireland. There were two routes, one from Penmaenmawr and the other from Abergwyngregyn. They were marked by wooden posts sunk into the sand, and met at a deep water channel about halfway across the Strait, where a ferry boat would be waiting for passengers to complete their journey at Llan-faes. This terminal was changed after the completion of Beaumaris castle, when the ferry service then terminated at The Green.

During the 13th century Llywelyn the Great, Prince of Wales, married Joan, the daughter of King John of England, and brought his wife to his home at Abergwyngregyn. But all was not well with the marriage initially, and Joan entered into a relationship with a courtier, William de Broas. Llywelyn discovered the intrigue and imprisoned William, later hanging him. Joan was imprisoned for a while, too, but eventually the marriage improved. When Joan died Llywelyn arranged her burial at the Franciscan Friary he had founded at Llan-faes, so her coffin was taken over Traeth Lafan and ferried to the Anglesey shore.

The Friary closed during the dissolution of the monasteries in the reign of Henry VIII, and Joan's coffin was disinterred and taken to Beaumaris parish church for a second burial. The heavy coffin lid was mounted in the south porch of the church, where it has been seen and admired by thousands of visitors over the centuries.

1. Joan's coffin in the south porch of St Mary and St Nicholas Church Beaumaris; 2. Joan's coffin lid; 3. The Menai Strait, from the heights of Garth Point Bangor; 4. Ghost's from the past on Traeth Lafan

Overleaf: Telford's bridge and the old quays

Caernarfon Market and Ferry

When the Romans came to Caernarfon, the Celts established a town – Yr Hendref (old town) – near Segontium – to sell supplies to the legions. The town was extended to its present site at the time of the princes with a palace down by the estuary. Throughout the centuries, trade was the backbone of the town's existence and Caernarfon markets – and fairs – brought the produce of the surrounding countryside onto the streets.

The original market was held in the open air in the middle of Stryd Fawr. A purpose-built market hall was erected later in Stryd y Plas, but all the cattle and stock would be sold in front of the castle on Y Maes Glas. Markets have been held since 1780 on Y Maes where the weekly Saturday market takes place today, with an additional market every Monday in summer.

A link with Anglesey was essential to Caernarfon and the history of the ferry to Anglesey goes back centuries.

The ferry became renowned in the eighteenth century. Caernarfon had become an important market town and the people of Anglesey were able to take advantage of its facilities. The ferry carried livestock and brought farm girls with their baskets of butter to sell in the market in Stryd y Plas. The prospective buyers were free to taste the butter first by digging out a dollop with their thumbs.

The ferry was a convenient link, but there were several mishaps during its history. In 1664, the large Abermenai boat was ready to land when there was altercation between the boatman and the loader concerning the payment of an extra penny. In the ensuing squabble, the boat drifted into deep water and capsized and some 80 passengers were drowned. At the time it was believed that the boat sank because it had been built of wood which had been stolen from the old Llanddwyn Abbey.

Between Caernarfon and the ferry landing stage at Tal-y-foel, there are dangerous sandbanks known as Y Traeth

The Anglesey was the ferry inn at Caernarfon

Gwyllt (*traeth*: sand; *gwyllt*: wild), and there have been several fatal accidents with the ferry failing to keep to the centre of the channel and ending up on Traeth Gwyllt. When the Menai Suspension Bridge was opened in 1826, the trade for the ferrymen at the eastern end of Afon Menai dried up, but the Abermenai ferry continued to link western Anglesey with Caernarfon until 1954. The old rowing boat was replaced with a steamer in the mid-19th century and in 1874 it was put under the control of the town council.

'*Fferi Bach Sir Fôn*' came to an end in 1954 and the last boat sailed from Caernarfon on July 30, along with seven centuries of history. These days, however, another boat takes visitors from Cei Llechi past Caer Belan to enjoy the beauty of both Anglesey and Arfon.

In Memory of Pigs

Before the bridges were built, farmers on Anglesey wishing to take their cattle and pigs to market crossed the Strait at its narrowest point where Telford was to erect his suspension bridge. The market was then held where the Antelope Hotel now stands.

This was sometimes a hazardous procedure as the timing had to be right, tides and currents were not always in favour. The animals had to swim across and often the swirling water would catch an animal unawares and it could be swept along, even as far as Bangor, being chased by men in boats trying their utmost to make them turn to swim against the current to the shore. Often animals were drowned.

Pigs received a slightly better treatment as they were allowed to rest briefly on a large rock close to the Anglesey shore, before attempting to complete their journey. This was the rock which was, later, flattened to hold the Anglesey stone pier of the suspension bridge, ever after referred to as Ynys y Moch (*Pig Island*).

There is a rock off the southern shore of Llanddwyn Island, Craig y Moch, which has a story.

At the end of the 19th century the Strait was busy with shipping, many of the vessels sailing to Liverpool. A pilot was usually available to guide them over Caernarfon Bar, but when the steamship *Monk* began to sail from Porth Dinllaen to Liverpool with a cargo of live pigs the captain decided to make the journey through the Strait without the pilot's help as he had done the journey before. This time the weather was against him. The ship broke up, all the crew drowned, and Caernarfon Bar was a sea of pigs and they were washed ashore.

In those days the annual autumn cattle market was held on land now occupied by the Antelope Hotel, on the Bangor side of the Strait. It was later moved to Porthaethwy, close to the Anglesey Arms Hotel.

Today Ynys y Moch is the resting island where the first stone of Telford's Menai Suspension Bridge was laid on the 10th of August 1819

A bridge had been contemplated several times before Telford's plan was accepted, but all were refused because they did not allow for the passage of ships with tall masts. Telford recognised the problem and designed his road deck to be one hundred feet above the water. At last, access and egress was made easier.

Stone for the bridge piers was quarried at Penmon and brought to the Strait in coasters. It was unloaded at the tiny islet at the east end of Porthaethwy village from where a rail had been laid down to the shore opposite Ynys y Moch, and dragged along in trucks by horses. The Anglesey pier was to be built on Ynys y Moch.

After 1826 when the bridge was opened to traffic, Porthaethwy assumed a new importance – and a new name. As 'Menai Bridge' it became a small town, a convenient stopping place for travellers using Telford's London to Holyhead road.

Ynys y Moch is now a quiet rock once more. The noise of objecting cattle is only a dream.

An aerial view of the suspension bridge

Ferries across the Strait

Mention has already been made of the earliest crossing of the Menai Strait, from the mainland to Llan-faes, and later to The Green at Beaumaris.

Since the 13th century there have been several ferries operating at various places along the twenty kilometres.

Some of the ferry boats must have been large. There is a record of one being overhauled and supplied with eleven oars. The larger boats took horses and luggage, even a dismantled coach as well as passengers.

The unpredictable weather and high tides could cause problems and accidents. There is a record of the Porthaethwy ferry having capsized, but one woman passenger made it to the shore because she was wearing a capacious petticoat which acted like a sail!

At the south western end of the Strait the Abermenai ferry carrying fifty passengers returning from a market in Caernarfon also capsized, all being drowned.

The ferries at this end of the Strait were kept busy with taking workmen from Anglesey to Felinheli and Caernarfon from where they would be given transport to work in the slate quarries. The men stayed in the quarry for several days, sleeping in the 'barracks' at Deiniolen and returning to Anglesey on the ferry at the end of a few days shift.

Some of the ferrymen were unique characters. The Garth ferry was once operated by a husband and wife team, the Parry family. The husband was well built and good at his work, but his small wife had a temper. On one occasion she was berating him while crossing the Strait, but the poor man had enough, stripped off his jacket, and dived into the water, leaving his wife to complete the crossing herself.

This ferry, during the 19th century was sometimes worked by the Parry's daughter, Grace. She had the strength of her father – and her mother's temper. It was said that Grace hated the English unless they tipped her, then her attitude would change.

The remains of a Moel-y-Don ferry with Felinheli across the Strait

MENAI HOTEL, Foel Ferry, Brynsiencyn, Anglesey.
Proprietor, H. BERNARD

One traveller who wrote of his experiences along the Strait, told how this happened to him. He thanked Grace on leaving the boat, and gave her a tip. She took it, wished him well, and shook his hand until almost dislocating his fingers.

After the bridges had been built, the Holyhead road in use and also a new road from Porthaethwy to Beaumaris, the need for the ferries ceased except for those taking men to work and their wives to Caernarfon market. These lasted a little longer.

In the latter years of the last century they became a tourist attraction, but now they have disappeared.

1. Menai Hotel, Foel Ferry from Brynsiencyn to Caernarfon; 2. Moel-y-Don Ferry which linked the Llanedwen district with the mainland at Y Felinheli; 3. Tal-y-foel ferry jetty at Abermenai

Ynys Gorad Goch

Those approaching Anglesey over the Menai Suspension bridge in the direction of Holyhead often stop in one of the two laybys on Telford's London to Holyhead road to appreciate the stupendous view across the Strait to the mountains beyond. They are also attracted by the green island with its white house and tower which hugs the coast below. This is Ynys Gorad Goch (the island of the red weir).

The tidal patterns in the Menai Strait, and the rocky sea bed, make it an ideal area for weir fishing. Fish are swept into the weir when the tide is high but cannot escape. Then the fisherman comes along to retrieve his catch.

There are several weirs along the fifteen miles of the Menai Strait.

Weir fishing at Gorad Goch has provided a livelihood for many over the years.

The property is, in reality, an island divided into two by a narrow channel, now crossed by a causeway. It was originally Crown property, but passed into the hands of the Bangor Diocese, and the diocese held it for around three centuries.

While it belonged to the church, a small room in the house came to be known as The Bishop's Room where bishops of Bangor would visit to spend time in prayer and meditation. A stone embedded in the wall near the window bears the initials and date 'I.R.1808' believed to refer to one of those bishops.

In the early days fish from the weir was supplied to monasteries in the area and some sold at local markets. Herring was cured in the tower.

During the 1800s the island was sold into private hands. Sometimes the property was occupied by tenants who paid a rent. Those tenants gained a livelihood by fishing the weir, and selling their catches.

When Telford's London to Holyhead road had been completed, a pathway was made through the woodland on the estate opposite the island, which made access much easier. Previously the only way had been by boat from Porthaethwy. This path led from the main road to a place on the shore opposite the island. Only a small

Ynys Gorad Goch

rowing boat was needed for the crossing from there.

The Madoc Jones family, who were once tenants, lived there over three generations. Then it was regarded as an idyllic place for a home – but, was it? The three boys in the family had to go to school, and did so at the Beaumaris Grammar school. Father would row them to the shore early in the morning, they would scramble up the path to the road, walk (or run) down to Porthaethwy then catch the school bus. And the journey in reverse in the afternoon. this, five times each week.

Father would fish the weir twice a day, depending on the tides – spend time curing herring, and selling his catches. At the end of the afternoon the boys would need to be met to bring them home.

During the summer the lady of the house would have an extra chore, as she provided 'whitebait teas' for visitors. These visitors, too, would use the path to the shore where they would ring a bell fastened to a tree, to summon a boat. They would be served whitebait, brown bread and butter and a pot of tea in the Bishop's room before returning. That would be an attraction to today's tourists.

At one period a Visitors' Book was kept on the island. It showed evidence of some well-known visitors, including a member of the royal family of the day, and David Lloyd George's wife and Megan, their daughter.

As one would expect from such a site, there was plenty of bird life. Writers over the years have mentioned flocks of terns, which would bombard anyone working outside. One of the Madoc Jones family would always carry a stick which he used to attack terns who attacked him. The lady gardener employed by an owner in the 1960s would always wear a strong straw hat to withstand any aerial activity. This was the lady who created a lawn at the front of the house, and surrounded it with shrubs which would withstand the foreceful weather to which Ynys Gorad Goch was subjected. And she also planted a herb garden near the tower.

Ynys Gorad Goch may appear idyllic on a pleasant summer day – but was it?

After the Menai Strait had been spanned by Telford's Suspension bridge, diarist Francis Kilvert, who had been staying in Bangor, went along to see it. He walked along the new road out of Porthaethwy, enjoying the views as he went, and met an old man who was ready to talk to a stranger.

'How would you like to live in that house, summer and winter, all the year round?' asked the old man, pointing to Ynys Gorad Goch. 'They live like fighting cocks there, they have a weir and catch all the fish.'

But local writer David Senogles, whose book *Ynys Gorad Goch* was published in the 1960s, thought otherwise. He wrote of the hardships endured by the families living on the island before many of today's facilities were available.

The landing stage at Ynys Gorad Goch

A Sea Route to Ireland

The last battle of the Civil War was fought in Beaumaris in 1646. It was an important port for the Royalist campaign throughout the conflict. The Bulkeley family supported Charles I and held the castle in his name but it was eventually taken by the Parliamentarians.

After Cromwell's final victory, he himself began to see Beaumaris as a useful location for his bloody and cruel campaigns in Ireland. Once again, the countryside of Anglesey was deprived of corn and cattle in order to feed armies.

Craftsmen, merchants, drovers and publicans flourished as a result of the increase in commerce. Judges and solicitors came to Beaumaris Court, which was built in 1614 and customs officers and excise men came to the port to try to catch some of the numerous smugglers who were active in this part of Anglesey. The 18th century was a period of high taxes on tobacco, spirits and tea, and since the Isle of Man was beyond the aegis of the English crown until 1765, the island was used as an enormous warehouse for contraband.

Naturally, Beaumaris and its bay were ideally placed to receive smaller boats which would distribute such goods.

Since the route to Ireland still meant crossing Traeth Lafan and waiting for the tide to cross the Menai to Anglesey, travellers created much of the commercial activity in Beaumaris. The ebb and flow of the tide forced them to tarry awhile – four miles of Traeth Lafan were under water for eight hours out of every twelve, so there was always a demand for hotels and taverns for travellers in Beaumaris. Some of the present-day public houses date back to that period – the George and Dragon was originally built in 1410, and the existing building dates back to 1595. The Olde Bull's Head was a big coaching inn, dating back to 1472. The Liverpool Arms was built in 1700.

The town was essential to the postal service from England to Holyhead and to Ireland as the government in London paid more and more attention to what was

The Old Court House, Beaumaris

happening in the 'Emerald Isle'. Beaumaris had its own postmaster from very early days – one of the publicans usually – but by 1718 the post road had been diverted to the ferry at Porthaethwy thereby causing a decline in the traffic on the route through Traeth Lafan and Beaumaris. The town post office lost its status and from then on, the erstwhile principal town of Anglesey also went into decline. It became even more inaccessible in 1826 when Telford built Pont y Borth (*Menai bridge*) – although a new route had been forged along the shores of the Menai to connect Beaumaris with Porthaethwy by that time.

Under the 1765 Anglesey Turnpike Act, the road from Holyhead to the Menai Strait was improved, and a stagecoach service between Shrewsbury and Holyhead, the port for Ireland, was established in the following years. By 1808, the mail route through Betws-y-coed increased the pressure on the ferry at Porthaethwy. The calls grew for a permanent bridge across the Menai Strait.

Despite the fact that an attempt to establish a wooden bridge across the Menai had failed in Parliament in 1786, by 1815, because of increasing pressure on the part of the Irish, an act was passed authorising the Holyhead Road Commissioners to spend money to build a bridge across the Strait. A certain Thomas Telford was appointed to oversee the work, and his famous 'high fortress over the depths' was opened in 1826. Telford was also given responsibility for improving the main road from London to Holyhead as well, and on completion, this would be the renowned A5. A local man, Siôn Jones, a civil engineer from Rhosmor, Llangwyfan, was one of the engineers who assisted Telford in securing the chains that supported the Menai Bridge, and as a result Telford gave him the responsibility of overseeing the building of the Conwy suspension bridge.

The old quay at Porthaethwy

Courts of Law and Order of the Gallows

Although Beaumaris declined as a town for travellers and commerce at the beginning of the 19th century, for several generations it continued to be Anglesey's principal town as far as administration and the law were concerned. It was the principal town of Anglesey until 1889.

Beaumaris Court is in the square in front of the castle entrance and is an experience in itself, having been restored to its former glory and opened to the public. The Great Sessions were held there from 1614 onwards and it was still in use as recently as 1971. There is a very entertaining exhibition showing the oppression of impoverished inhabitants by the legal apparatus of the state. Some were deported to Australia for fairly paltry offences and Welsh speakers were abused. One example of a poor man being oppressed by the principle of 'protection of property' which is a feature of English law is that of Hugh Hughes in 1786 who was whipped publicly through the streets of the four towns of the island for stealing food.

There were plenty of real wrong-doers around, of course. Amongst them were Lladron Crigyll (*Crigyll robbers*) from north-west Anglesey. Afon Crigyll flows into the sea to the north of Rhosneigr, through boggy land and sand-dunes. Ships used to be lured to their doom in this area by lanterns being hung around the necks of cattle, giving the impression of a safe harbour to sailors to shelter from a storm. The ships would be smashed on the rocks and caught on the sandy beach – then the local wreckers would attack them, killing the sailors and passengers, stealing their property and their cargo. In 1742, there was a celebrated case in Beaumaris when Lladron Crigyll were successfully captured, after an attack on the *Loveday and Betty*. Unfortunately, taking advantage of the fact that the judge was drunk, one of the four in the dock accused the ship's captain of deliberately beaching the ship, and since the court was full of acquaintances and former offenders, the defendants were allowed to go free.

Beaumaris Gaol

When capital punishment was called following a court case, a gallows would be erected on Penrhyn Safnes (known as *Gallows Point* in English) to the west of Beaumaris harbour. Visible for weeks from the busy sealanes, the corpse, left to rot on the gallows, would serve as a warning to boatmen and sailors who travelled back and forth along the Menai. Nowadays there is a shipyard on Penrhyn Safnes.

Today, the Court offers visitors an opportunity to see an exhibition of legal attire and paraphernalia, to see the prisoner's cell and follow his/her steps to the dock, to stand in the dock itself and to learn about some of the most famous criminal cases which were heard in this building.

The original town gaol was situated in one of the castle towers. Later, a prison was built on the green by the sea but this was pulled down to build the fashionable Victoria Terrace and the Bulkeley Hotel in the 1830s. The purpose of the Georgian architecture was to create a special image for the town, to show that it was worth dropping anchor in its harbour to pay a visit.

The new gaol which was built in the town's backstreets has a different image. However, in its day, it was considered to be just as splendid. The building, designed by the architect Joseph Hansom, was erected in 1829 and it was a template for prisons of its time. There are detailed notes giving information about the prisoners and their crimes and today, one can visit the cells, the chapel, the workrooms, the treadmill which drew water up to the tank, the hard labour yards and the condemned cell. It is a building full of sad memories and stories; the coldness and hardness of its walls and the ironwork illustrate its dark history, a piece of history which sticks in the imagination.

According to the standards of the period, ordinary folk would be given extreme punishments for offences which are now considered to be petty crimes. Poaching especially was an offence against the landlord and was seen as a challenge to his authority – although the spoil was often only a rabbit or a pheasant or two for a starving family. In August 1849, Robert Weston of Beaumaris received a month's hard labour in this prison for poaching and was fined £10 at the end of the month. The following month, Richard Jones, again from the town, was given three months hard labour for the same crime. During the Victorian Era, poaching was the fourth most common offence in the Courts of Petty Session on the island.

The most famous prisoner to be kept here was Richard Rowlands, the last man to be hanged in public on the prison's wall having been found guilty of killing his father-in-law. That was in 1862, with a large crowd of people from every corner of the island present to witness the hanging. Before the drop, he insisted that he was not guilty and cursed the clock tower. Taking into account later evidence, including his wife's words on her deathbed, historians now believe that he was not the murderer and according to tradition, this is why the hands of the clock's four faces have never kept the same time since.

The gaol was closed down in 1878 but reopened as a heritage centre by Anglesey County Council.

At the other end of the Menai Strait, s well as ruling the people, their punishment was another key element of the foreign regime at Caernarfon. Originally, there was a prison in one of the castle towers, but since the middle ages, the court and prison have been located in Pen Deitsh under the shadow of the castle on the landward side. The present-day buildings were built in 1853 and 1863, and include a residence for the judge and lawyers. The law has been administered from here for over 700 years and on top of the building, there is a statue of Justice with a blindfold over her eyes, the work of a craftsman from Porthaethwy.

Next door to the courts there is the old gaol, which is now part of the County Offices. The police station was housed here from 1850 and there are extensive cells in the cellar. One of the towers on the town wall forms the back of the building. This was part of the prison at one time, with a big treadmill in the yard in front of the tower, and the tower itself being used as a platform for the gallows until 1850. The 'advantage' was that the audience the other side of the wall could watch the condemned being hanged, even after legislation in 1832 prohibited the hanging of people in public places.

The last person to be hanged in Caernarfon gaol was William Murphy, who was condemned for killing Gwen Ellen Jones, his ex-lover, in 1910. When the bell tolled in the church of Santes Fair to announce his death, the bell rang out twice and then fell silent. It was later discovered that the clapper had fallen off at exactly that moment – after serving continuously for 170 years.

The court archives are now kept at the County Archives near Doc Fictoria. They are unique throughout Wales for their antiquity, dating back to 1541 – only in one other county in England are there records which predate them. The earliest document records a man being hanged for stealing hay worth 20 pence.

The old court at Caernarfon

A Wreck and a Lighthouse

During the 1830s there was a regular passenger service between Liverpool and northern Wales, passing through the Menai Strait. The company running the service used an early, unseaworthy vessel, *Rothsay Castle*, manned by an unruly ignorant crew and an incompetant master.

One day in August 1831 one hundred and fifty passengers boarded the ship, which ran into stormy weather in Liverpool Bay, shortly after leaving. The wind was so strong that it hindered progress, and the passengers demanded that the captain should turn back to port. But he remained in his cabin and refused, telling the protestors that there was no need for panic. All would be well.

Rothsway Castle continued to battle with the strong gale, and more passenger protests were met with the same refusal.

As darkness fell, the ship came close to Ynys Seiriol, struck a sandbank on Traeth Lafan, sheered off only to hit Dutchman's Bank and become fast.

The captain and his mate came on deck and as they did so the funnel and mainmast fell on them and killed both. At the same time the vessel broke in pieces and one hundred and thirty lives were lost, the remainder being picked up by a lifeboat and taken to safety.

The story struck horror widely, and a petition was started to provide a light at Penmon Point.

Trinity House built the lighthouse at Trwyn Du a few years later.

James Walker, who designed Trwyn Du lighthouse included some features not seen before on his earlier designs for buildings elsewhere. Instead of the iron railing around the gallery, he built both gallery and safety wall of stone. A toilet was introduced. The building stood on a decked base which allowed for sewage to fall directly into the sea.

1. *Traeth Lafan;*
2. *Trwyn Du lighthouse and Ynys Seiriol*

Four silent train spotters

When Robert Stephenson made plans for his Britannia Railway Bridge across the Menai Strait, he intended that a tall statue of Britannia should be mounted on top of the bridge. This would be seen for miles around, and along the Strait. This would be the finishing touch. But it was not to be, as rising costs of building did not leave money to spare.

Instead, Stephenson commissioned architect and sculptor John Thomas to provide four huge lions, two to be placed at each end of the bridge, these to emphasise the strength of the design and construction.

John Thomas was then also working on decorative items for the new Houses of Parliament, under Sir Charles Barry. He worked on stone carvings in the House of Commons, and was also responsible for statues on the north and south fronts.

The massive stone lions were made in eleven pieces each from Penmon stone. Each measures twenty five feet six inches long, and weighs eighty tons.

These now famous stone figures first 'spotted' a train in March 1850 when the bridge was formally opened.

Over one hundred years later they were to see the bridge catch fire and in 1970 its rebuilding, with an open rail track and road deck above to carry the A55 expressway.

Today those lions are not often seen as they lie hidden out of sight by travellers. One wonders what local people of 1850 thought of them. *Y Bardd Cocos*, the folk poet from Porthaethwy wrote these famous lines to applaud the lions:

> *Pedwar llew tew*
> *Heb ddim blew,*
> *Dau yr ochr yma*
> *A dau yr ochr drew!*

> (Without any hairs,
> Four lions fat;
> Two over this side
> Two over that!)

The famous huge lions that rest beneath the new road over the Britannia Bridge

Construction of Robert Stephenson Britannia Tubular Bridge May 1849; 2. The re-modelled Robert Stephenson Britannia Tubular Bridge, after the disastrous fire on May 23 1970; 3. The original Menai Suspension Bridge opened 1826, and reconstructed in 1938–39 to its present day format

Strait snippets

(paragraphs translated from the Welsh newspaper, *Y Clorianydd*, issues of the year 1900, which reflect a different world . . .)

The year began with an epidemic of influenza which spread through the villages along the Strait. 'There have been complaints for some weeks that this unwelcome visitor is staying rather too long. It was particularly noticeable during the Week of Prayer, when many were not able to attend as they were incarcerated at home.'

A startling announcement regarding the Menai Suspension Bridge was made during February. 'The Council was invited to send three members to meet Arfon County Council to consider buying the Menai Suspension Bridge by the two counties jointly. Opinions were divided, the chairman casting his vote, deciding against the issue.'

Magistrates' courts on the island were kept busy with a variety of cases. 'At Porthaethwy a case by the agricultural Board was heard, when Lord Anglesey was accused of breaking the law (The Importation of Dogs Order 1897) by not keeping a dog imported from Germany apart in accordance with licence and omitting to muzzle it. His Lordship was fined £1 on both charge. A similar fine was imposed on John Dicens, the hunt keeper, who was in charge of the dog.'

As spring advanced, there was growing interest in the development of Beaumaris marina. 'The pleasure steam yacht belonging to Sir Richard Williams Bulkeley, the *Vague* arrived on Tuesday from Marseilles. Also the steam yacht *Cestra* belonging to Mr J. Johnson Houghton on the following Saturday on her maiden voyage. Mr E. K. Muspratt's well known yacht, the *Wonderful*, left the Menai for Hoylake where, it is said, she will be broken up and the lead used in a new vessel which Mr Muspratt is building.'

This was the year when Beaumaris held its first bicycle parade. Riders wore fancy dress. The newspaper reported the occasion as an unparalleled success. The procession was led by a pony and cart pulling a

tandem through the streets, much to the enthusiastic reception by a large crowd.

The Menai Strait saw its usual share of wrecks and tragedies in 1900. 'Three Newborough men went in a small sailing boat across the Menai to Caernarfon. It was considered they were not in a fit state to make the crossing.' Someone on shore noticed that the boat capsized, and immediately he and a helper set sail to the rescue. The three men were eventually saved and treated on shore by two local doctors.

As winter approached, the price of coal was giving concern. 'Beaumaris. The weather continues very wet and cold in these parts, and to make things particularly dispiriting, the price of coal has risen very high remembering that it is 28/- a ton at present, and it is said it will rise even higher. Is there not room to despair in face of the coming winter? It is to be hoped things turn out better.'

The ferry jetty from Newborough to Caernarfon

A name remembered over four centuries

There can be only few living along the Anglesey shore of the Menai Strait who do not recognise the name of David Hughes, emblazoned as it is on the large comprehensive school at Porthaethwy. This David Hughes was born in Anglesey during the middle of the 16th century. He received higher education at Magdalen College, Oxford, then went to Grays Inn, London, and eventually secured a post as manorial steward of Woodrising, Norfolk, a prestigious post which he retained until his death in 1604.

But although he lived far away from his native Anglesey, he was especially concerned about the education of the poorer classes of its society.

During the middle of the 16th century a number of 'free grammar schools' had been founded by men with the same concerns. Friars School in Bangor was one instance, this was founded in 1557. David Hughes determined to found a similar school for poor children whose parents could not afford to pay school fees.

In 1603 he set about his task, using the existing small building close to the moat surrounding Beaumaris Castle. The Beaumaris free grammar school was born. At the outset, this was to benefit the poor children of Anglesey families, although, as the years passed and education became wider, this was to change.

Religious changes brought their problems to David Hughes's style of education, as initially the school was for children of families connected with the established church.

In spite of many problems, the school flourished, and lasted well into the twentieth century, until comprehensive education became the norm. Then the school was integrated into the new system of education and became part of the large comprehensive school at Porthaethwy where the name of David Hughes was perpetuated.

How David Hughes would have marvelled at all these developments!

1. Date of 1603 carved in stone above the door of David Hughes School; 2. Tablet on the wall of the former school building, now a community centre in Beaumaris; 3. The Beaumaris moat; 4. David Hughes School in Beaumaris

THIS · TABLET ·
WAS ERECTED
IN GRATEFUL MEMORY
OF
· DAVID · HUGHES ·

THE GENEROUS FOUNDER
AND BENEFACTOR OF THE
BEAUMARIS GRAMMAR SCHOOL
ON THE 300TH ANNIVERSARY
OF ITS FOUNDATION.
· 1603 – 1903 ·

The Industrial Strait

In the past the Menai Strait was a busy place. Ships, large and small, were built at several yards along the shores. When the slate industry at Bethesda, Llanberis and Nantlle grew, slate was exported from Bangor, Felinheli (Portdinorwig in those days) and ships bringing everyday needs, before the roads were improved, filled their empty holds with slate for Liverpool, Dublin and farther away, wherever it was to be used for roofing the fast growing towns and cities.

In Porthaethwy the Davies family were building ships of sizes. The largest would cross the ocean and return, their holds full of timber from the American forests. The timber would be stacked in a warehouse on shore, to be used in future shipbuilding.

There was a tiny port opposite Felinheli which was known for its special use of slate. This was Pwllfanogl, where slates were cut and polished and mounted in wooden frames, for use in schools. Slate pencils were made here, too – and how they squeaked when used by the children! School slates sold well in those far off days, in Wales and in England.

There is one piece of history lying in the water of the deep channel – a ship piled with slate which was wrecked during the 15th century.

When there was industrial activity at Pwllfanogl there was also a bacon factory, a building where chicory from Colonel Strapleton Cotton's fields was treated, a flour mill and smaller workshops. Tea and cakes were available for workers at a tea shop.

Today all is quiet at Pwllfanogl. Some of the buildings have been converted into living accommodation, used by visitors.

1. La Marguerite *arriving at Porthaethwy on her farewell voyage. At her final departure there were touching scenes with rockets fired in salute. Beaumaris also gave her a good send-off with the Town band playing 'Auld Lang Syne'; 2. Passengers pouring off* La Marguerite *in August 1905. They arrived at 2:40pm and were allowed an hour ashore to spend money in the ships, rea-rooms and pubs. During the Edwardian era an average of 30,000 passengers landed at Porthaethwy each summer*

1. The old stone Pier at Porthaethwy;
2. St Trillo, *a motor vessel 150 feet in length with accommodation for 568 and designed to cater for short sea excursions between Llandudno and Porthaethwy and Amlwch;*
3. Passengers disembarking from La Marguerite *at Porthaethwy in 1905. She was the largest excursion steamer of her time, registered to carry 2,077 passengers*

Until his death a few years ago artist Sir Kyffin Williams had his studio here.

During the Second World War industrial development of some importance took place on the ancient Fryars site at Llan-faes. This was done by the Hawker Siddeley Group. Flying boats used in the war effort were maintained here, as access to the shore and the Strait was easy. Products were also made at the factory, like reflectors for pontoons.

As time went by, mergers happened. One of the sizeable orders to one of the new firms was to create a great number of bodies for double decker buses of London Passenger Transport.

Today the road from Beaumaris to Penmon which passes one of the old slipways is quiet. The days when Anglesey workers flocked to Llan-faes to earn a living are past.

Slates to Roof the World

The slate trade was the major contribution of the Menai shores to the Industrial Revolution. Caernarfon was a key port during the first half of the nineteenth century. The quarries at Dinorwig and Nantlle between them produced some 40,000 tonnes of slate in 1800 and there was a total of 248 ships in Caernarfon to carry them all over the world.

The local slate industry received a tremendous boost in 1842 when most of the city of Hamburg was destroyed by fire. Two local quarry owners travelled to Germany to urge the inhabitants to re-roof their houses with slate – emphasising how the fire would not have spread from one building to the next with such ease had they not been thatched. This created a new market not only in Germany but also in every other industrial town in Europe and America.

The port at Felinheli was developed to export slates from Dinorwig in 1819 and the trade of Caernarfon slate ships continued to flourish – in 1844, 85,388 tonnes were exported from Caernarfon alone.

The quarries of Dyffryn Nantlle provided the cargo for the ships of Caernarfon. The quarries of Hafodlas, Tal-y-sarn, Pen Bryn and Dorothea were in operation early in the nineteenth century, and after completion of the narrow gauge railway from Nantlle to Caernarfon in 1828, the town's importance increased and it became a centre for political, religious and educational activity in the county. Between 1830 and 1880, Cei Llechi was a hive of activity with hundreds of ships and men involved in exporting slates to all parts of the world.

Slates were exported from Caernarfon to every part of the island of Britain and a considerable trade developed with north America, particularly the cities of New York and Boston, and there was a huge demand for schooners for that trade. Over 200 ships were built on the river banks and in Doc Fictoria between 1758 and 1898. That dock was also the site of the Patent Slip (which is still to be seen today) where small ships could be hauled up to be cleaned and repaired. Emigration to America was also part of the activity at the

port of Caernarfon, with regular sailings for passengers to New York.

In 1922 the Welsh Highland Railway was opened, running from Porthmadog through Eryri to Dinas just outside Caernarfon. It closed down in 1937. The track has now been completely re-laid from Caernarfon (a few metres from Cei Llechi) to Rhyd-ddu. It is hoped that it will run all the way to Porthmadog by 2009. This journey passes through some of the most spectacular scenery in Eryri.

Although the export of slates may have come to an end, the craft of slate dressing can be seen at Inigo Jones' slate works in Y Groeslon (8 km outside the town on the A487). There is a shop, a café and an interesting exhibition tracing the history of the industry in the area.

As the slate quarrying industry grew,

①

②

③

Porth Penrhyn on the eastern side of Bangor on the mainland was flourishing. The Penrhyn family used wealth gained in the slave trade to open and develop Chwarel y Penrhyn in Dyffryn Ogwen. A quay was built at the mouth of Afon Cegin in order to export slates to markets in Britain, Ireland and the rapidly developing new world. The small port was named Porth Penrhyn, and in 1801 an iron tram track was constructed from the quarry at Bethesda to the port, a revolutionary invention at the time.

By the 1850s more than 100,000 tons of slates were being exported annually from the quay, and during the same decade 14 boats were launched at Bangor. Porth Penrhyn was also the site of a number of industries which had sprung up because of the slate industry, including the production of writing slates in wooden frames for the schools of the time. Many of the original buildings that housed these various industries can still be seen at Porth Penrhyn today, and perhaps the most interesting is the circular lavatory erected by Lord Penrhyn for the convenience of his workforce. There was room to enthrone ten at a time in this 'roundhouse', and no doubt it witnessed many an interesting debate!

1. *Porth Penrhyn; 2. Penrhyn slate tip;*
3. *The 'Roundhouse'*

Three local men remembered

There can be few coastlines in Wales like that of the Menai Strait. Here, within only a few miles, are memorials to remind us of three local men.

Sailing west from Ynys Seiriol the tall pencil-like column standing high on the hill behind Beaumaris catches the eye. This is dedicated to Sir Richard Bulkeley Williams of Baron Hill, Beaumaris, who died in 1875. It was erected by his 'tenants, neighbours and friends', says the plaque on its base. This Sir Richard was keenly interested in agriculture and was 'energetic and munificent' and not averse to contributing to enjoyment in life.

A few miles farther along the coast, now overlooking the Britannia Bridge, stands what is known locally as the Anglesey Column. It was financed by the first Marquess of Anglesey's countrymen of the counties of Anglesey and Caernarfon and was erected in memory of his military activities. He commanded the cavalry in Spanish wars and was second in command at Waterloo, where he lost a leg.

On the shore, hidden from the road but close to the parish church of Llanfairpwll, there is a smaller statue. This depicts Nelson. It was erected by the Marquess's brother, Rear Admiral Clarence Paget. This, it is said, was done to highlight the service of the Royal Navy. It is regarded as the first to be made of concrete. When built it was intended as a navigational aid, guiding sailors towards the dangerous waters of the Swellies. The Rear Admiral designed and had a hand in its making.

Today, Nelson appears as a lonely figure.

The famous Marquis' Column, which reaches a height of 91ft above Craig y Ddinas, the site of an old Welsh fort, looks down on these shores. The statue was built

1. Standing high above Beaumaris, Sir Richard Bulkeley Williams' Column; 2. The first Marquess of Anglesey Henry William Paget's Column, at Llanfair PG, completed on the 24 March 1860; 3. Nelson on the shore of the Menai Strait by the Britannia Bridge – 'England expects that every man will do his duty'

in 1817, two years after the battle of Waterloo, to celebrate the role played by Henry William Paget, the Earl of Uxbridge, in that famous battle, and who lived at Plas Newydd nearby. Uxbridge was Wellington's second-in-command, and he lost his right leg towards the close of the battle, but still lived to the ripe old age of eighty-five. There are 115 steps to the top of the monument, designed by the architect from Chester, Thomas Harrison, and from the top you can see spectacular views of Snowdonia. The poet from Porthaethwy wrote these memorable lines to greet the Marquis and his column:

> Y Marcwis of Anglesey
> Dorrodd ei glun,
> Tasa fo'n torri'r llall
> Fyddai gynno fo'r un;
> Y Marcwis of Anglesey
> Â'i gledd yn ei law,
> Fedar o ddim newid llaw,
> Pan fydd hi'n bwrw glaw!

(*The Marquis of Anglesey broke his thigh, if he broke the other, he'd be high and dry: the Marquis of Anglesey with his sword in his hand, he can't change hands, when it rains where he stands!*)

Today, the first Marquis' home, Plas Newydd, is owned by the National Trust, and this splendid building has a long and colourful history. Originally it was owned by the Penrhyn family from Bangor, but at the end of the 18th century it was acquired by Henry William Paget. The house was extensively restored from 1793, mainly by the renowned architects, James Wyatt and Joseph Potter.

If the most famous member of the family was the hero of Waterloo, another who brought a great deal of colour to the mansion's history was Henry Cecil (1875-1905), the fifth Marquis. He formed a drama company and turned the family chapel into a splendid theatre. Some of London's finest actors took part in his productions, and the Marquis would perform his own 'butterfly dance', but in 1904 the 'mad Marquis', as he was known locally, became bankrupt, and died within the year in an expensive hotel in Monte Carlo. The stately home is worth a visit to see the famous mural, created between 1936 and 1940 by Rex Whistler, or to enjoy a cruise on the Menai.

Plas Newydd

'Boys will be Boys'

This story begins in August 1877 when an industrial training ship, *Clio* arrived in the Menai Strait to be moored near to Bangor Pier. Over the next forty-odd years many teenage boys were to be trained here for sea-going careers. They came, mostly, from underprivileged families all over Britain. Some were orphans, others from families unable to give them the upbringing they deserved. Training on the ship was rigorous. The boys lived in close confinement, where the atmosphere was harsh.

Written records remain, but a collection of slate memorials in Llandegfan churchyard are a more public record of how life on *Clio* could affect the young trainees.

These memorials list the names of many boys who died while pupils or soon after the start of their careers, through a variety of illnesses – pneumonia, meningitis or tuberculosis and others through accidents which happened on board.

Boys fell from aloft during recreation time – it was common to play climbing the rigging. An Inspector spoke to a newspaper reporter about such an accident, shrugging it off with the comment 'boys will be boys'.

On another occasion a youngster died in hospital after being kicked by a group of three older boys who had bullied him, and injured his head. The local papers made much of the stories of accident and illness.

One inspector, however, spoke kindly of the captain and his wife, saying they could not be expected to watch over their pupils every moment of the day, even in such close confinement.

Bullying was only to be expected. In the case mentioned, the three miscreants who had bullied the new recruit to the school were expelled and each sent to a separate reformatory.

Local parents dealing with a son's misbehaviour at home would warn their offspring that unless they behaved better they would be sent to *Clio*. *Clio* came to the end of its life as a training ship in 1920 when it broke up in the Strait.

1. *Sleeping quarters for the boys on board the* Cli
2. Clio *at her moorings opposite Bangor pier in 19*

Flowers fascinated them

In 1861 a wealthy Cheshire barrister at law, William Massey, began to build a large house at Llangoed, near Penmon. By 1865 'Cornelyn' was completed, and William brought his family to Anglesey to make it their home. The views from its windows embraced the Menai Strait.

William had two daughters, Edith and Gwenddolen. The girls were encouraged to socialise with others in the neighbourhood, so they rode and partied, but they had their own interests, too. They painted and embroidered.

There was a small cottage on the 'Cornelyn' estate, hidden from general view, and this the girls converted into their studio.

Flowers were an obsession. Gwenddolen was slightly lame, so could not roam the fields, as did her sister Edith. Edith would return to the cottage after a walk, carrying bunches of wild flowers, which would then be sorted before Gwenddolen would decide which to draw and paint. Edith collected information about the flowers, their growth, where they were found. The paintings were kept carefully in volumes, very many of them over years, along with the information.

It was not until the sisters had died – during the 1940s and 1960s, that these volumes came to light when a sharp eyed curator saw that they were to be auctioned at Crewkerne in Somerset. At the time Anglesey County Council was building a museum and gallery at Llangefni – now Oriel Ynys Môn.

A successful bid was made for the large collection of volumes and the drawings restored and framed to become a valuable part of Anglesey's artistic treasures.

Not only are Gwenddolen's pictures displayed frequently, but Edith's informative notes are an important addition to knowledge of Anglesey's flora.

1. Cornelyn home of Edith and Gwenddolen Massey, photographed about 1870;
2. Cornelyn in the grip of winter snow.
By permission of Oriel Ynys Môn, the Isle of Anglesey Museum Service

Penmon Priory

Without doubt, the most influential saint in this part of Wales was Seiriol. His ecclesiastical centre was in Penmon and the remains of the original 6th century buildings can be seen there at the south-eastern tip of Anglesey.

A number of carved stones and Celtic crosses from the age of the saints have been preserved. The church and the monastery at Penmon received patronage from the Welsh princes including Owain Gwynedd and Llywelyn Fawr. The remains of Seiriol's original cell and well (below) are still to be seen on the site.

Penmon Priory and its dovecote and (above) a carved Celtic cross

A famous musician

Sometimes you could see him walking down the road towards Porthaethwy, a nondescript figure often wearing a black hat and carrying an umbrella. This was William Mathias. There was nothing about him to suggest that he was a musician, famous throughout the world.

William Mathias was born in south Wales. As a child he was a prodigy as far as music was concerned, playing the piano at three years of age and beginning to compose at the age of five.

He had his formal music training at University College Aberystwyth, going on to the Royal Academy of Music in London. He returned to Aberystwyth as a lecturer, later going to Bangor as senior lecturer in the music department which led on to his appointment in charge of the department.

William Mathias composed for individual instrumentalists, orchestras and choirs – with a particular interest in church music. And he composed an opera, to much acclaim.

The Royal Family knew of Mathias as he wrote an anthem to be sung at the wedding of Prince Charles and Princess Diana.

Universities around the world knew of William Mathias. He was presented with honorary awards by some of them, including two doctories.

Shortly before his death he was honored by receiving the CBE.

William Mathias lived in a house slightly above the road from Porthaethwy to Beaumaris, whose windows gave wide views of the Menai Strait.

William Mathias left north Wales a valuable bequest – he was founder of the prestigious music festival held annually at St Asaph.

William Mathias

Another training ship arrives

Conway was a wooden-wall ship with tall masts. She was moored in the Mersey between Liverpool and Birkenhead until 1941 when it was feared that she might suffer from enemy air raids during the Second World War. She was moved to the Menai Strait to find a new home was moored between Bangor pier and Glyn Garth. Educating boys for a career at sea became very popular, and space for the boys on board ship difficult as a consequence. The captain favoured a shore base which could offer certain facilities, so a search began. Eventually an agreement was struck between *Conway* and the Marquess of Anglesey who offered a piece of land on the estate in a convenient position. At the beginning this was a campsite and playing field, until a purpose-built building was erected later.

But this meant yet another move for the ship – one done with a certain amount of trepidation. Tugs were used to guide her. Passing under the suspension bridge was a real problem, as there was very little space to spare between the tall masts and the road deck. But all was well and *Conway* moored between the bridges.

In 1950 it was decided that *Conway* needed a re-fit and this was to be done in Birkenhead. Again, tugs were employed, to guide her into a safe channel. By this time a new captain was adamant that he could guide the ship over the Swellies and into the open sea, in spite of warnings by experienced seamen of the dangers. But strong currents had their own way, and the ship was driven on to rocks between the bridges, unmovable, and damaged. She caught fire and soon broke up, a sorry wreck. The remains still lie below water.

The school continued for around twenty years, using the shore base.

A tragic end to a great ship on April 14, 1953 while being towed from her moorings at Plas Newydd for a re-fit at Birkenhead, one of the tug's tow ropes parted and she ran aground near the Menai Suspension Bridge

Aerial views of heritage either end of the Menai Strait – Segontium Roman fort near Caernarfon and Porth Penrhyn which used to export Dyffryn Ogwen slates

An Anglesey export

In the days when puffins frequented Ynys Seiriol in great numbers, they were caught, pickled and exported to the English markets. How would you pickle a puffin? One Anglesey housewife, Margaret Wynne of Boderwyd, kept a recipe book in which she included instructions on how to pickle puffins. It read like this . . .

'Make ye puffins cleane as soon as ye take ym and draw ym, then let ym lye in water a whole night. Wash ym clean in yt liqour and turn up there leggs and parboyle ym in water and salt for halfe an houre and as ye take ym out of ye hott water shake ym in cold water and sett ym enwaeisse to run all Night. Next morning lay ym flat on there breasts in a dry cloth and crush them a little until they be thoroughly dry, with a knife and lay ym on there breasts in a vessel. Take a pottle of white wine and as much white wine venegar and 2 pottles of Alagar, 2 mace, ginger and 2 peper ye mace and ye peper must be bruised, and ginger sliced yn boyle all these a little in ye liqour with a handful of salt and when it is thoroughly cold clear it and take ye spice that is in ye bottom and throw between every lay of ye puffins in ye vessell as ye pack em up in ye liqour and put a round slate or board to keep em under water and stop up ye vessell close yt no wind get in. This liqour and spice is a fit proportion for six dozen.'

A puffin decoration on a Beaumaris street sign

Celebrations

Massive new projects such as the Menai Suspension Bridge and the Britannia Railway Bridge have their problems. Designers have to work out their plans in advance, and when these plans are successful there is excuse for celebration.

One of Telford's greatest problems was how to fix the sixteen chains to hold the road in position. If his method of fixing the first was successful it could be used on them all.

The first, heavy chain was laid on a raft which was towed into position when weather and tide were right. Then the action of hauling this manually lifted it to where it could be bolted successfully. This was done to cheers from a large crowd assembled to watch the process. But those cheers turned to gasps of horror as three workmen were seen to walk swiftly along the chain from one side to the other. Celebration? Not the kind of celebration an angry Telford approved of, and next morning the three workmen were reprimanded for their foolhardiness.

The remaining chains were hoisted and attached in the same way.

When it was the turn of the final chain to be secured a platform had been built to hold a local band who, when the signal was given, walked down to the centre of the chains where they played the national anthem to loud cheers.

Another celebration, but this was arranged with care.

The official opening of the bridge came when the Irish Mail crossed on its way to Holyhead, followed by two coaches containing dignitaries, and what must have been a very proud and happy Thomas Telford.

Nearly twenty five years later the Britannia Railway Bridge was completed. The great iron tubes which were to carry the railway across the Strait were built on the mainland shore before they were floated into the water and lifted into position between the massive stone piers. Many of the workers had come from England and settled in a shanty-fashion

The famous chains of the world's longest suspension bridge when it was built in 1826

settlement nearby, to be augmented by local Welsh people. The engineering section of the Chester to Holyhead Railway decided there should be a special occasion to mark the success of the project so far, and a concert was planned to be held inside the huge centre tube prior to its removal from the shore. All the workmen and their families were invited. This was to be a memorable occasion.

Seating was placed the length of the tube, internally and the area was brightly lit. Singers from Bangor and Caernarfon were invited to perform. Local newspapers estimated that between seven and eight hundred residents from the local communities on both sides of the Strait enjoyed 'a wonderful occasion'.

The official opening took place when Robert Stephenson and passengers made their first railway journey through the tubes and so forged another link between the mainland of Wales and Anglesey.

Overleaf: The Menai Suspension Bridge and the Carneddau mountains

Bangor – The City of Learning

During his revolt at the beginning of the 15th century, Owain Glyndŵr established the ideal of a University for Wales. By the latter years of the 19th century, this ideal began to become a reality, and a teacher training college, *Y Coleg Normal,* was established in Bangor in 1862. Because of its convenient location and rail and road links, Bangor was chosen as one of the sites for two new university colleges in Wales. On 24th August, 1883 it was announced that Bangor would be home to the new University College of North Wales.

But government policies alone did not lead to its foundation. The farmers and quarrymen of the region also wanted their children to enjoy a better standard of education. A committee was established on every *'ponc'*, or workplace on the quarry face of Chwarel y Penrhyn, to raise money for the University. When the college opened in 1884, 3,000 quarrymen marched through Bangor to mark the occasion.

The college opened its doors at the beginning of the Michaelmas term 1884, on the site of the old Penrhyn Arms hotel on the highway into Bangor. At one time this was an inn 'equal to any in the Metropolis' according to Dr Johnson. And the coming of the University ensured that Bangor would never grow old, with a new generation of students streaming into the city every autumn. The doorway to that first building still stands, looking across at Porth Penrhyn, and on the first day 58 students registered to study at the college. By the end of the century there were 300 students at Bangor, and new and larger premises were required.

The City Council supplied land for a new site, and the architect Henry Thomas Hare was appointed to design the building. In 1911 the University moved to the new, imposing building on the hill not far from the old 'Roman camp'. Since then the 'college on the hill' looks down on Bangor's bustling streets, creating a unique contrast with the old cathedral in the valley below.

With the University College and the

Bangor University College

Normal College, and Friars Grammar Schools and the Girls' Grammar School all within a stone's throw of each other, Bangor's old educational tradition had been re-established by the beginning of the 20th century. The city was also an important centre for religious education, with the Baptists' College and the Bala-Bangor College next to each other, again in Bangor Uchaf. Generations of gifted students have graduated and enjoyed their time at Bangor.

The suburb of Bangor Uchaf developed as the centre of the students' studies and activities, and although this part of Bangor has seen many changes over the years in terms of its resident population, it is still at the heart of student life, a patchwork of pubs and cafés and restaurants, with the occasional bookshop to fulfill educational needs.

1. The old Normal College; 2. The doorway to the Penrhyn Arms Hotel – site of the first university; 3. Coat of arms

The Eagle and the Dragon

At the south-western end of the Menai Strait, the town of Caernarfon is marked by its massive castle, with Tŵr yr Eryr (*Eagle Tower*) announcing its position from afar.

Caernarfon has always been at the hub of nationalistic tendencies, in promotion and protest.

At no time was this more pronounced than in the early to middle years of the last century.

Early in 1932 the government was requested to allow the Welsh flag, the red dragon on its green and white background, to be flown side by side with the Union Jack on Tŵr yr Eryr – this to commemorate St David's Day.

The request was refused.

This was enough to prompt four nationalists (two solicitors among them) to raid the castle and remove the Union Jack. One of the raiders was held in Caernarfon gaol for the day.

By lunchtime a group of students at the University in Bangor heard of the raid and its outcome, and decided to add their protest. They sped to Caernarfon and entered the castle legitimately, paying the entrance fees, and made for Tŵr yr Eryr where they cut down the Union Jack, cutting it into small pieces, each keeping a piece for himself as a memento. They ran down to the lawn, joined hands, and sang the Welsh national anthem to the joy of a crowd of sympathisers who had gathered there.

The police were there, too, but made no attempt to arrest anyone. After the cheers had died down the students walked back to the bus to take them back to college.

Sympathies for the protest must have run high, as no more was heard from the police nor the University about the matter.

Today the Welsh Dragon flies freely from the top of Tŵr yr Eryr.

Caernarfon castle's Tŵr yr Eryr

A man in a women's world

Down below the Marquess of Anglesey's Column a roadside sign announces the village of Llanfairpwllgwyngyll. Today it is a busy place, visitors arriving in coaches from all over Britain, reading with interest the toll charges still to be seen on the tollhouse at the entrance of the village.

This was the site of the first tollgate from Porthaethwy which travellers would meet on the island after crossing Telford's Menai Suspension Bridge.

This was also where they would be reminded by their tour guide that this village was where the first branch of the Women's Institute in Britain was set up in 1915.

It was founded by a man who lived locally.

The man was Colonel Stapleton Cotton, an ex-army officer who had served in the Zulu War at the beginning of the last century. He suffered paralysis in his lower limbs when his tent was struck by lightening during a heavy storm, so retired from service and came to live in a house on the estate of his nephew, the fourth Marquess of Anglesey, on the road to Brynsiencyn from Llanfairpwllgwyngyll village.

The Colonel was a man of many interests and did not allow his injuries to curb his enthusiasm.

He set up a co-operative to ensure that the marram grass weavers of south Anglesey found markets for the mats, baskets and other useful articles they made from the tough grass which grew on the sand dunes. He encouraged local gardening so that food could be produced from what local people grew for themselves. He opened a bacon factory and an egg collecting point and was busily occupied on various county committees.

When the branch of the WI was set up, members made him and his dog, Tinker, who accompanies him everywhere, honorary members.

With the building of the Britannia bridge in 1850, the railway ushered in a huge increase in the number of visitors to

1. Toll House, and Women's Institute Hall on the A5 at Llanfairpwll; 2. WI

the island, and as usual the inhabitants of Anglesey made the most of this new market.

As the story goes, it was a tailor from Porthaethwy called Thomas Hughes who came up with the long version of the name of the village of Llanfair Pwllgwyngyll, and to begin with, this was just some kind of family entertainment. All the elements in the name can be seen from the top of the Marquis' Column – the church of Saint Mary in Llanfair, the white hazel pool on the Menai, which is opposite the 'fierce whirlpool', called Pwll Ceris (*pwll*: pool) on the Menai. Facing the pool is the island of Tysilio, but there is some doubt if *gogo* means cave and *coch* (red) might stem from the island of Gorad Goch, an important fishing point at one time, which is the island on the Menai exactly between both bridges. The long version of the name was posted on the first railway station on the island, and immediately became an attraction to the passengers who would roar past towards Holyhead.

On paying a visit to Llanfair Pwyllgwyngyll, there is much more to the village than the name itself. One of the first houses after crossing the Britannia bridge is 'Coedlys', a small bungalo that was the home of the artist and architect Richard Huws. He designed the 'triban', which is the symbol of Plaid Cymru, the Party of Wales. Some of the area's other artists are Wilfred Mitford Davies (1895-1966) who was the main illustrator for Welsh children's magazines, and Sir Kyffin Williams, whose studio is down at Pwllfanogl on the shores of the Menai.

The church of Saint Mary is also down by the Menai, and in its cemetery there is a massive column commemorating the deaths of fifteen men who were killed while building the Britannia bridge between 1846 and 1850. Also buried in the cemetery is Sir John Morris-Jones, the Welsh poet and scholar who was inspired by the views of the Menai. After marrying, Sir John lived at Tŷ Coch in the centre of the village, opposite the station. His father, Morris Jones, and his brother, W. R. Jones, kept the old 'Siop Stesion' which is now part of the Penrhos Arms tavern. Tŷ Coch is still considered to be an exceptionally beautiful house, and to a large extent Sir John himself drew up the designs.

There are a number of other interesting buildings in Llanfair PG,

St Mary's, Llanfair Pwllgwyngyll

especially the Thomas Telford toll-house built at the beginning of the 1820s. Next door to the Turnpike there is another historic building, the home of the Women's Institute, the 'W.I.' At the height of the Great War in September 1915, the first branch of the W.I. in Britain was established in Llanfair PG. To begin with the women met in a small cottage in the gardens of 'Y Graig' in the village, but the organisation grew rapidly, and during 1920 they went to look for a larger building. Since an appropriate building was not available in the village, they bought the old 'Officer's Mess' from Kinmel Bay army camp near Bodelwyddan. The hut was re-erected in the garden of the Turnpike, and the members have met here regularly since 1921.

St Tudno (III) at Porthaethwy in 1953, certified to carry 2,493 passengers with a speed of 19 knots. She had replaced the La Marguerite in 1926 and sailed on the North Wales service each summer until her owners went into voluntary liquidation in 1962

St Seiriol (11) *passing under the Menai Suspension Bridge in July 1953, one of her cruises around Anglesey, a distance of 150 miles and advertised as 'the finest one-day sail in Britain'*

Boys who worked at the end of the 1800s in the slate factory for dressed school slates in wooden frames, and slate pencils, at Pwllfanogl factory. Boys between 16 and 18 earned a salary of 9 pence a day for a 6-day week, with work starting at 7:30am to 6:30pm

1. *Snowdon arriving in Menai Bridge from one of her regular pre-war excursions from Llandudno to Caernarfon where passengers were allowed two hours ashore; 2. The tiny port of Pwllfanogl; 3. Relics of the Saunders-Roe site at Llan-faes, Beaumaris*

What of the future?

As readers will have seen, the Menai Strait has had its industries over the centuries. What of its industrial future?

Today, Strait water is being used in an imaginating active way by a new company, Anglesey Sea Salt Ltd. based at Brynsiencyn. It all began some years ago when two graduates from the University in Bangor created a small oyster farm which developed into a fish and game business.

Then the Sea Zoo appeared on the Anglesey shore, which has become an important feature of the local tourist industry.

The healthy growth of some of the inhabitants of the great tanks proved the cleanliness of the water.

A simple experiment with a pan of boiling sea water which, as it cooled, produced brilliant crystals, was to be the foundation of Halen Môn (*Anglesey Sea Salt*).

The business of production started in a small way, before the present 'factory' was built near the Zoo. It was an instant success.

Today Anglesey Sea Salt is sold all over the world – it will be in demand for as long as food is consumed.

What other new developments will take place in the future?

Anglesey Sea Zoo and Halen Môn

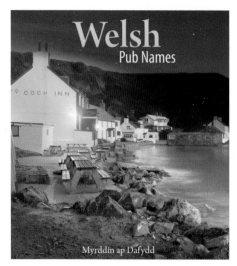

Welsh
Pub Names

Myrddin ap Dafydd

COMPACT
CYMRU

COMPACT
CYMRU
– MORE TITLES;
128 PAGES
£5.95
FULL OF COLOUR IMAGES
AND CONCISE WRITING

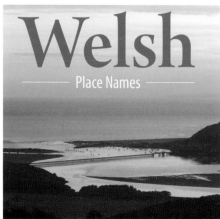

Welsh
— Place Names —

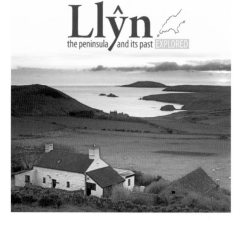

Llŷn
the peninsula and its past EXPLORED